FENG SHUI
TIPS FOR A
BETTER
WEALTH
FAMILY LIFE LOVE
CAREER CREATIVITY
HEALTH

 DAVID DANIEL KENNEDY
Foreword by Professor Lin Yun

STOREY
BOOKS

*The mission of Storey Communications is to serve
our customers by publishing practical information
that encourages personal independence
in harmony with the environment.*

Edited by Aimee Poirier and Elizabeth McHale
Cover design by Paul Perlow
Text design and production by Cindy McFarland and
    Susan Bernier
Line drawings by Sarah Brill
Calligraphy by Professor Lin Yun
Indexed by Nan Badgett/Word•a•bil•i•ty

The information in this book is true and complete to the
best of our knowledge. All recommendations are made without guarantee on the part of the author or Storey Books. The
author and publisher disclaim any liability in connection
with the use of this information. For additional information,
please contact Storey Books, 210 MASS MoCA Way, North
Adams, MA 01247.

Storey Books are available for special premium and pro-
motional uses and for customized editions. For further information, please call Storey's Custom Publishing Department
at 1-800-793-9396.

Printed in Canada by Transcontinental Printing
10 9

Library of Congress Cataloging-in-Publication Data

Kennedy, David (David Daniel)
    Feng shui tips for a better life / by David Kennedy.
        p.   cm.
    Includes index.
    ISBN 1-58017-038-2 (pbk. : alk. paper)
    1. Feng-shui. I. Title.
BF1779.F4K46 1998
133.3'337—dc21   98-5958
                                                     CIP

Contents

Dedication

To those who use Feng Shui knowledge to improve their lives.

Acknowledgments

The author gratefully acknowledges:

Feng Shui teacher and mentor Professor Thomas Lin Yun.

Sarah Rossbach, for bringing Professor Lin's teachings to America.

Crystal Chu, Ho Lynn Tu, and the staff of the Yun Lin Temple.

Feng Shui teachers James Moser and Seann Xenja.

Arisha, for helping me with my Feng Shui journey.

Foreword

Tigers swirling like wind,
Dragons curling like clouds
They seem so unreal, yet so true.
Clear water; lush green,
All things seem high-spirited.
Where karma begins and ceases,
I shall reveal this great knowledge to thee.

— Lin Yun

AN ANCIENT CHINESE PROVERB SAYS, "When decorum *(li)* is lost, one has to retrieve it from *ye*." As the word *ye* can mean either "folk culture" (as opposed to elite culture) or "foreign country" (as opposed to homeland), this proverb has two distinct meanings. First, while certain customs and practices, such as *Feng Shui,* may have faded in elite circles, they are vigorously kept alive in folk culture. Second, even though Buddhism was suppressed in its indigenous India, it prospered in faraway Cathay, enriching and being enriched by Chinese civilization. Examples of both types are abundant in the history of comparative cultures.

Speaking of the first meaning of the proverb, although various cultures name the same phenomenon differently, what we call "Feng Shui" may have started with the genesis of human society. Even primitive societies knew how to use their knowledge to harmonize with nature. Feng Shui thus represents both the living and lived experiences of human beings. We should not cling to it without reason, but rather endow it with new significance in the light of time and advances in human knowledge. Some Chinese intellectuals have sanctified Western knowledge at the expense of their traditional cultural heritage. Those with a superstitious view about Western science unfortunately look down upon Feng Shui — even though it represents traditional Chinese intuitive wisdom.

Since 1973, I have lectured on Black Sect Tantric Buddhism throughout the United States and the world. Chinese folk Feng Shui is a subject I have studied closely. I always advise my friends and students not to make themselves higher than others by slighting people with different views. To those who portray Black Sect Tantric Buddhism as a "superstition," or a "side door" (unorthodox), I say that I am accustomed to these criticisms and use them to learn, but I am totally at ease with what I represent.

I hold that a superstitious belief is still a belief, and a "side door" is still a door. Which, after all, is the right way, and which is the wrong way? The earth is round, so who is on the right side and who is on the left? Right may be wrong; wrong could seem right. It hinges on one's perspective and the context in which one lives. I once wrote a poem to convey this:

> *The universe is wondrous, while the*
>   *earth is round.*
> *So who's standing behind, and who's in*
>   *the foreground?*
> *To separate left, right, center, side,*
>   *may be nothing but presumption.*
> *Even awakening and confusion are*
>   *between reality and illusion.*

Speaking of the second meaning of the proverb, different cultures can respect and learn from each other. Black Sect Tantric Buddhism (in its four generations) has integrated the Tibetan

Bon religion, Indian Buddhism, and different branches of Chinese cultures including the *I Ching* and Yin-Yang thought, developing a unique perspective about life and the world. When it came to the United States, it reached its fourth generation, which I represent.

Since the West has surpassed the East in the spirit of practice and the pursuit of research, I brought Feng Shui to the Western world to enrich it with modern knowledge. Someday we may take it back to the East. While fourth-generation Black Sect Tantric Buddhism is not restricted by modern science, it is open to scientific verification as a mutually enriching exchange of information.

I have established a Black Sect Tantric Buddhist School of Feng Shui, which is similar to and different from traditional Feng Shui schools. My school, like other Feng Shui schools, is embedded in the enduring Chinese traditions. They all try to provide a guide to help people create ideal environments for their homes and workplaces. This is Feng Shui. However, my school differs from others in three important aspects:

1. My school retains the essence of traditional Feng Shui and the basic principles of geomancy. However, we emphasize learning the Eight Trigrams *(ba-gua)* and using the Ever-Changing Eight Trigrams *(ba-gua)* when adjusting Feng Shui. We give equal importance to the shapes of objects *(xing)* and to the intentions of the person *(yi)*. We do not think of the compass *(lo-pan)* as the only essential tool for reading Feng Shui. We note the directions of objects, but emphasize their Mouth of Chi and relative positioning.

2. We have added modern scientific knowledge to interpret Feng Shui. In addition, we advocate both mundane and transcendental solutions to adjust Feng Shui.

3. We have combined Feng Shui with spiritual studies and folk religions.

Because of these features, my Black Sect Tantric Buddhist School of Feng Shui is accessible and useful to many Westerners. There has been a surge of interest in the study of Feng Shui in recent years. Most notably, Sarah Rossbach, a distinguished scholar, has published four books in collaboration with me, which have been generously received and translated into many languages. Wherever I go on my lecture tours, I feel the enthusiasm that people have for Feng Shui, including leaders from many walks of life, scholars, and believers and priests of other religions. I believe that Black Sect Tantric Buddhist Feng Shui has not only been accepted by people in Western countries, but has also exerted a strong impact on architecture, interior design, gardening, city planning, and real estate. It provides important counsel for the development of commercial buildings, airports, harbors, and residences. Eastern wisdom has crossed national borders at this level.

Mr. David Daniel Kennedy is one of my formal disciples in the United States. He is a learned and compassionate person. Having benefited from Feng Shui, he has devoted his energy to writing this practical book in order to explain Feng Shui for others' benefit. He starts with the basic principles of Feng Shui and expands into a wide range of topics: from wealth to love, from health to family and children, and then to fame, knowledge, and more. The beginner can profit directly from this easy-to-understand book, while those knowledgeable in Feng Shui can also gain a clear, systematic understanding from a fresh perspective. Most importantly, Mr. Kennedy has provided more than 100 transcendental solutions from the Black Sect Tantric Buddhist School that would ordinarily remain undisclosed. I would like to recommend this highly practical and interesting book to any reader who shares our common karma. And to Mr. Kennedy, I extend my congratulations on his achievement.

— Professor Lin Yun

Translated by Professor Chin-Chuan Lee.

"Feng Shui"

相好不如命好
命好不如心好
心好不如運好
運好不如氣好

一九九七年重九題勉

DAVID 甘乃迪賢契

從龍山人 林雲

"Good Chi" (This proverb is translated in English on page 11.)

Welcome to Feng Shui

*It's not just that you create your house,
it's that your house also creates you.*

WELCOME TO FENG SHUI, the Chinese art of auspicious placement. You are beginning to discover a 3,000-year-old, yet very practical, way to balance your environment and improve your life.

This book is about changing your environment to create good fortune, prosperity, and a better life. Within these pages, you will find more than 200 specific and powerful ways you can change your home and office to enjoy your life more. Whether your desire is to increase your wealth, enjoy better health, or simply to have a more comfortable home, you will find many techniques to fit your needs.

If you are a beginner in Feng Shui, you will learn a simple yet powerful process of changing your relationship to your home. If you've already experimented with Feng Shui and would like to add more skills to your repertoire, you will find many new, effective ways to apply Feng Shui to your life.

For centuries, Feng Shui has improved the fortune and luck of its followers, while creating a host of welcome life benefits. By using Feng Shui methods, you can change your life experience in significant ways: increasing your luck, having more happiness, and gaining more control over your circumstances. Using your living space to create your wishes, dreams, and desires may be a new way of looking at life, but it is one that you will find enjoyable and richly rewarding.

How to Use This Book

You can use this book in either of two ways:

1. As a text. Read all the way through the book, noting which tips interest you the most. This method can give you more of an overall understanding of how the tips work and which ones apply to your needs.
2. As a how-to manual. To get started quickly with the tips that will help you immediately, go directly to the chapters that interest you most. As you apply the tips and experience the improvements in your life, your needs and desires may evolve and change. You can always come back and read sections you have skipped.

Getting the Most from This Book

1. Read chapter 1, "Feng Shui Principles and Concepts," to gain a basic understanding of how Feng Shui methods work.

Perspective

This book is written from the perspective of Professor Lin Yun's Black Sect Tantric Buddhist Feng Shui school. This system is very accessible to Westerners, yet contains techniques that create powerful results. The techniques taught in this book may differ from those of other Feng Shui schools, yet they are effective and easy to implement. Credit for the theories and techniques herein goes to Professor Lin Yun; please attribute any errors and omissions solely to the author.

2. Start a notebook for Feng Shui in your life. Start by writing down one to three areas of your life that you want to improve. Life areas to choose from in this book are Wealth, Love and Romance, Health and Vitality, Business and Career, Opportunities, Family and Children, Reputation and Fame, Helpful People and Friends, Knowledge and Self-improvement, and Special Situations.

Decide which changes you want to make in the life areas you have chosen, and make a written note of these desired changes.

3. Read the chapters that apply to the life areas you'd like to change. Jot down the tips best suited to your needs, abilities, tastes, and budget.

4. Next, read chapter 12, which includes tips for making your Feng Shui changes as effective as possible.

5. Apply the chosen Feng Shui tips as quickly as possible. Urgency and action help create momentum and change in your environment and your life. Check off each tip on your list as you go.

6. Watch for changes in your life, both sudden and gradual. Expecting and noticing the life changes you desire is a key factor in the process. You could see immediate and dramatic improvement in one area of life you're working on, and slower, more gradual shifts in another. As you observe your life changing in response to the Feng Shui you've done, you will be able to see if more work is necessary in any area of your home or life.

7. When you feel ready for more Feng Shui, you can reassess your life areas, choose additional tips to follow, and jump in again!

As you begin applying Feng Shui to your home and life, you will notice a shift starting to take place in your awareness. Your environment will begin to "come alive" to you in new ways as you interact with your space more consciously and intuitively. You'll start to get your "Feng Shui eyes," recognizing which features of your home have been limiting you and which you can improve.

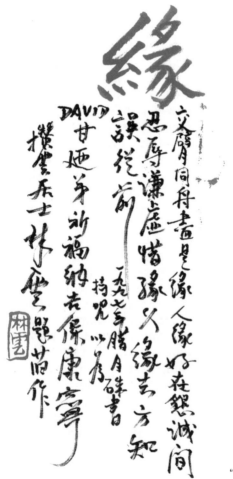

"Destiny"

1
Basic Feng Shui Principles

THIS CHAPTER INTRODUCES the Feng Shui concepts and principles that will give you a basic understanding of Feng Shui: its definition, background, and theory. When you have completed this chapter, you will understand how to read your home's floor plan so you can begin applying the Feng Shui tips to your life at once.

What Is Feng Shui and How Does It Work?

Feng Shui is the art of using arrangement and placement to improve your life. It is a way of manipulating environmental factors to enhance the life energy of the environment and improve your destiny. Life energy, known as *chi* to the Chinese, is the basic force that animates all living things. Your own flow of chi will improve and strengthen as you apply Feng Shui principles to your life.

The term Feng Shui *(fung shway)* means "wind-water." It comes from a Chinese proverb describing the most desirable place to live. It says:

Where the wind is mild and the sun warm,
The water clear and the vegetation lush

Feng Shui's aim is to create harmony between man and nature, placing you in the very best location and circumstances possible.

Feng Shui Master Professor Lin Yun gives another definition of Feng Shui:

Feng Shui is the method people naturally use to choose and locate, build and construct, or adapt and change their working and living environments for maximum health, wealth, and well-being, according to the knowledge then available.

This definition says that humans in all cultures and times have used "personal environmental engineering" to improve their lives whether or not they had a specific term like *Feng Shui* to describe their practices.

In Chinese tradition, Feng Shui is only one of the key factors affecting our lives. According to Professor Lin, these are the chief life factors for success, in order of importance:

▸ Fate or destiny
▸ Luck
▸ Feng Shui
▸ Accumulating good deeds
▸ Education
▸ Others

Of course, the best life circumstances come from having beneficial features in all of these areas. However, Feng Shui is one life factor over which we have a significant degree of control. By adjusting and improving our Feng Shui, we have the opportunity to improve our luck and nudge our fate toward a more propitious course.

A Brief History of Feng Shui

This ancient art and science has been practiced and refined in China for thousands of years. Many methods have arisen, only some of which are still practiced today.

Feng Shui originally began as the study of optimal places for grave sites. This practice was based on the belief that graves were "houses" for the ancestors. People believed that auspiciously locating the graves of their ancestors and rulers helped to ensure future success for their family and nation.

This practice developed into the study of the most powerful locations and conditions for royal palaces and religious temples. Soon wealthy landowners became interested in acquiring Feng Shui advice for their own homes.

Priests and sages, many of whom were a combination of minister, doctor, astrologer, and all-around soothsayer, were the original practitioners of Feng Shui. After an extensive site examination, these energy wizards would give detailed advice on how, when, and where to locate and construct the home. Eventually, more of this knowledge became common among the general populace, and secular practitioners began performing Feng Shui as a business endeavor.

Feng Shui Schools

Over the last 6,000 years, two main methods of practicing traditional Feng Shui emerged: the Compass Method and the Forms Method. **The Compass Method** practitioner would take an astrological reading for the master of the house to determine the best direction for the house to face. Compass Feng Shui masters used a special Feng Shui compass (*lo-pan*) to pinpoint the ideal setting and orientation of the home. Additional aspects of the building process, including proportion, dimension, the time and date to begin construction, and many others, were calculated based on compass readings, numerology, and the positions of heavenly bodies.

The Forms Method approached the same basic goals from a different angle, with an emphasis on reading and interpreting visible and invisible shapes and energies inherent in the local landscape. The landforms were symbolically interpreted as representing mythical shapes, including dragons, tigers, phoenixes, turtles, and others, each having multiple levels of significance. Additional factors considered included the nature and flow of water features, local weather patterns, and the views seen from each direction. According to the specific needs of the landowner, the chosen site's landforms would be in harmony with the building's purposes.

Although most of today's traditional Feng Shui masters practicing in Hong Kong, Taiwan, and the Western Chinese communities use a combination of the traditional Compass and Forms methods, other Feng Shui methods have also emerged over the years. These include the **Symbology Method,** by which everything in the environment is seen and interpreted as a symbol for understanding energy, and the **Reading Chi Method,** which emphasizes feeling the building's energy through the body, senses, and emotions to provide an intuitive Feng Shui understanding for the occupants.

Ultimately all schools and methods of Feng Shui have the same aim — to create balance between man and his environment.

Besides these traditional methods, a more recent school of Feng Shui has been introduced by Professor Lin Yun called **Black Sect Feng Shui**, which originates from the Black Sect of Tibetan Buddhism. It is eclectic, featuring Indian, Tibetan, and Chinese teachings, and Western approaches to ecology and the environmental sciences. Black Sect Feng Shui combines several schools of Buddhism, Taoism, folk methods, and theories of Professor Lin into a large body of powerful life-changing techniques. Using them in your life effectively does not require you to adopt any foreign belief system or ideology, but simply to have an open mind and the desire to improve your home's energy.

The Red Envelopes and the Oral Feng Shui Tradition

Since the Black Sect Feng Shui system is an oral tradition, cures are made even more powerful when they are taught orally. Traditionally, Black Sect teachers ask their students or clients for "lucky" red envelopes, each containing money, in exchange for spoken Feng Shui cures. The red envelope practice honors the teachers of this information and helps to safeguard the power of the tradition.

How Does Feng Shui Work?

Feng Shui works by balancing and harmonizing the chi, or "life force energy," that flows in and around our houses, yards, and offices. Feng Shui theory says that each building receives energy from the surrounding environment, and that energy circulates within its environment. The combination of these environmental energies and their characteristics is the "chi state" or energetic health of the building. The early energy masters of China researched and recorded the energy patterns that contribute most to overall balance for living, leading to the accumulation of Feng Shui knowledge.

Every minute of every day your home environment is either supporting and uplifting you or having a draining and de-energizing effect on your life energy. This is true whether or not you are consciously aware that it is happening! This is the inner truth of Feng Shui. Enhancing your home's energy has a direct and immediate impact on your own energy and life. Your personal energy is the basis of your life. Enhancing this energy is a powerful way of maximizing your destiny.

The Theory of Chi

One of the most basic principles of Feng Shui is the theory of chi. *Chi* is a Chinese word with many meanings, including breath, spirit, vitality, and life energy. Other cultures also have terms for this vital energy, including *ki* (Japanese), *prana* (Indian), *mana* (Hawaiian), *life force* (Western), and many others. In this book, the terms "chi" and "energy" refer to the same phenomenon.

Chi is the inner force that pulses through all living things, invisibly providing them with energy, motion, and vitality. A healthy, strong, and balanced person has "good chi" or healthy chi. A weak or sickly person's chi is described as poor or lacking.

Chi and the Body

As Professor Lin Yun states, "Your chi is the real you, and your body is the vehicle for your chi." This chi or life energy is what animates your body, gives color to your face, causes your limbs to move, and creates the sparkle in your eye. When a person dies, what leaves the body is the chi, the "empty" body is left behind.

According to Chinese medical theory, chi flows through meridians or pathways in the human body. The meridians carry vital life energy to the organs and limbs. Traditional oriental medicine is a system for interpreting the health of the body by observing its state of energy. All levels of the body — blood, lymphatic system, nervous system, and skeletal system — are considered to be superficial to chi. They all depend on chi for their functioning.

Chi and the Earth

Just as chi energy flows through our bodies, chi energy also flows within the earth. The veins or meridians of the earth's energy are called dragon lines. Where the chi is near the earth's surface, the land is energetic, lush, and rich in vegetation; where the chi circulates far below the earth's surface, the land is barren and dry.

Chi in Our Homes

In our homes, chi flows throughout the structure based on the geometry, layout, colors, and

---

The Importance of Chi

Having good physiognomy (facial structure) is not as good as having a good fate
Having a good fate is not as good as having a good heart
Having a good heart is not as good as having good luck
Having good luck is not as good as having a good flow of chi
— Professor Lin Yun

---

materials used, and other factors that constitute the structure. The arrangement of rooms, proportions of the design, and the relationship of the house to the land create energy channels and patterns within the home. The reason that balancing your home's energy flow is important is that the chi in your home is one of the most powerful factors that continuously conditions and affects your own personal supply and flow of chi.

Chi flowing in a person (right). Chi flowing within a house (below).

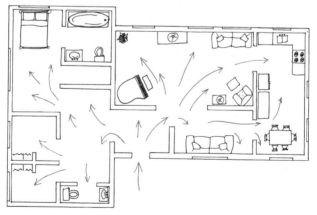

Types of Chi and Chi Cultivation

There are many different types of chi in the universe:

Chi	Description
Natural chi	The energy of nature, plants, and animals
Heavenly chi	The energy of the sky and solar bodies
Human chi	Your energy — the internal energy of humans
House chi	The energy that circulates in the house
Societal chi	The energy of the nation

Your House as Body

Metaphorically, your house is your "second body." How you treat this second body has a very real impact on your physical body and the events that occur in your life. Every element in your home contributes to its chi condition. Just as one's physical body can look beautiful, fit, and well dressed, yet still harbor internal illnesses, so can a home be well constructed and expensively decorated, yet have many hidden energy problems that debilitate and hinder the lives of its residents.

The mission of Feng Shui is to match the home's chi to the chi of its occupants. The chi in your home is not some "mysterious force" that occasionally and vaguely affects your destiny. The chi of your environment has a deep organic relationship with your own chi. These flows of energy continuously affect, condition, and create each other.

All these types of chi affect our lives. Some may be difficult for us to offset or change, such as natural chi or societal chi. However, your personal chi is one flow you can cultivate or gradually build and strengthen. Some of the methods Professor Lin Yun says people can use to cultivate their chi are:

Chi Cultivation	Method
Natural chi cultivation	Spending time in nature
Spiritual chi cultivation	Spiritual endeavors, such as prayer, meditation, and reading scriptures
Chi transmission	Receiving energy healing from qualified healing practitioners
Self-cultivation	Study, discipline, and self-improvement
Feng Shui cures	Environmental chi cures and remedies for the home and workplace

Feng Shui is only one of the categories of chi cultivation. The highest life benefit comes from using as many of the chi cultivation methods as possible; they work together to create overall improvement in your personal chi and life.

All Feng Shui schools, regardless of their orientation, focus on maximizing chi — balancing it, aligning it, increasing it, and deflecting its negative aspects wherever possible. Feng Shui practitioners are artists and technicians of the chi flow, using any means at their disposal to weave human and environmental chi into patterns of nourishing energy, which feed and protect every part of your life.

Your Feelings: The Key to Sensing Chi

It is not necessary to generate a belief in chi or to master the ability to sense it in order to receive great benefit from Feng Shui. Chi may not be easy to see, but you can definitely feel its effects. Your personal chi is nothing more than your own energy — it is not complicated or difficult to sense. The simplest and easiest way to sense your own energy is to be in touch with the way you physically and emotionally feel at any given time. As you become used to paying more attention to how you feel, you will become more attuned to the subtle effects the environment has on your own energy. As you adjust your chi with Feng Shui changes, your ability to sense or feel your chi and the chi of the environment will improve steadily.

New Environments

An easy way to tune into the chi of different environments is to pay more attention to the way you feel in your body immediately upon entering a new environment. This physical and emotional feeling is your body's response to the environmental chi you are experiencing in the new space. This simple personal feeling can give you a good impression of a building's energy character. How do you feel when entering certain neighborhoods in your city, your friends' houses, or different rooms of your own house? Asking yourself this question can give you important information about the chi in any space.

The period immediately after you enter a new place is when you will be most sensitive to its energy. This is when it will be most obvious how this space feels different from the place you just came from. After you've been in a space for a few minutes, your system begins to adjust to its energy. You can "get used to" how it feels and become somewhat less aware of its energy characteristics as time goes on. If this happens, pay close attention to see how you begin feeling immediately upon entering the same place the next time. (Even if you become less aware of how you feel in a space, you are not being less affected by its energy.)

Reading the Chi of New Environments

Your body gives you messages whenever you are in a space. All it takes to "read" the chi of a space on a basic level is to pay attention to these messages. This technique is very simple and easy to do. You will get better at it with time and experience. Don't discount your feelings! They tell you the truth. Practicing this simple technique will make you more sensitive to the environment and how it is continuously affecting you.

The energy of your home, including its colors, shapes, materials, geometry, location, and arrangement, has continuous and profound influences on your personal energy state, affecting you simultaneously in thousands of ways. Twenty-four hours a day, seven days a week,

---

Energy Flow as Metaphor

One good way to think about Feng Shui is that the events that occur in your life result primarily from the state of your own personal energy flow. Even if thinking about "energy" and paying attention to feeling it are new to you, it is very helpful to practice these skills. Use energy flow as a metaphor for your life, and it can help you create much better Feng Shui in your home.

your environment broadcasts continuous and widespread effects on your chi and that of your family. You may not yet be aware of the majority of these effects.

The Power to Change — The Choice Is Yours

In Oriental philosophy, Feng Shui is one of the most important factors of life, contributing to health, longevity, and overall happiness. Your chi impacts and conditions your whole being, including your body, mind, emotions, and spirit. If your chi is depressed, your thoughts and physical energy will be depressed as well. If your chi state is stagnant, you will look and feel stagnant and stuck. If your chi is bright and animated, your body and mind will experience and project bright, lively qualities of energy.

There is no "magical switch" you can use to turn off or get away from experiencing Feng Shui effects. The only real options are:

▸ Continue being affected as usual by your current Feng Shui — for better or worse.
▸ Change your Feng Shui now to create a better and more powerful life.

The choice and the power rest in your hands! By using Feng Shui to improve your home's chi, you can greatly enhance your own chi. Your improved state of chi will automatically create new, more enjoyable emotions, feelings, ideas, thoughts, words, and events in your life.

Increasing Return with Feng Shui

As your personal chi becomes more balanced, your thoughts and decisions improve, your emotions become more stable and harmonized, and wonderful opportunities come to you. Other people begin to notice, and feel free to pass gifts and deals your way. Your increasing fortune reinforces your good feelings and positive chi, and a powerful, virtuous cycle is initiated. From this point of view, Feng Shui is a practical method of maximizing your destiny.

The process of doing Feng Shui through feeling the energy of your home, then selecting and performing Feng Shui cures based on your feelings of energy itself becomes a feedback loop. The more balanced the chi in your home is, the more balanced your personal chi becomes, leading you to even greater attunement to your environment's energy. You are increasingly aware of new possibilities — cures you can do to create even higher states of balance forever.

When you have done Feng Shui for several months, you may look back and marvel at the astounding changes occurring in your home and life. By paying attention to how things really feel and performing the simple cures in this book, a powerful process unfolds. As you change your space, it helps you receive the things you want and need in your life.

The Essential Reason for Feng Shui

The essential reason for doing Feng Shui is so the chi of your home can be more conducive to your growth, development, and success. By overhauling and tuning the flow of your home's energy with Feng Shui, you directly enhance and cultivate your own energy.

Symbolism of the Home: You Are Your House, Your House Is You

After chi, the next basic Feng Shui concept is symbolism. In the Chinese way of thinking, each part of your home symbolizes and relates to one or more life areas. Your main front door symbolizes *beginnings,* the bed symbolizes *rest* and *relationship,* and so on. Every part of your home relates to something in your life — these relationships are the underpinnings of every system of Feng Shui. This metaphorical way of looking at the world is vital to having a more intimate relationship with your home and its energy.

Your home is a basic expression of your life. Every aspect of your home reflects who you are and the condition of your inner and outer life. For example, your bed represents marriage or relationship in your life. Take a minute to think about the conditions surrounding your bed at this moment. How does it look? How does it feel? Is it cluttered, chaotic, and unclean? Or is it tidy and pleasant, reflecting order and balance? The answer will probably reflect something that is going on in your relationship life right now.

Of course, because multiple factors are affecting you, it is possible to have a neat bed-room and still have a chaotic marriage. This example points to just one of many Feng Shui factors affecting the life area of relationship. Other areas of your home and workplace also contribute to the success of your relationships.

The Theory of Relative Positioning

A key theory in Professor Lin Yun's Feng Shui system is the Theory of Relative Positioning, which states: "The closer a part of the environment is to you, the more impact it has on your chi." Therefore, the most powerful locations in which to place Feng Shui cures are those that are closest to you. The most powerful location of all for doing cures is your own body/mind complex. The environmental areas that affect you, in order of decreasing importance, are:

- You
- Bed
- Bedroom
- Home
- Yard
- Neighborhood
- City
- Nation
- World
- Universe

As you select your cures, keep in mind that the areas nearest to you, particularly your bedroom, have the most effect on your personal Feng Shui and energy.

The Mouth of Chi

The Mouth of Chi is the primary point where energy comes into your home. In the same way that the mouth of the physical body takes in food, air, and energy (chi), the Mouth of Chi of the house admits chi, people, and opportunities into your home and life. Each house has only one Mouth of Chi. This very important location is the main front door of your house. (The front door is the Mouth of Chi even if you don't use it very often.)

The Mouth of Chi is the literal and figurative beginning point for all things that occur in life and in your home. It is also the point that defines the boundary between "inside" and "outside" areas of your environment. If this location is blocked, all areas of life can suffer; if your Mouth of Chi is bright and full of positive energy, your life can be blessed and enriched.

By identifying your Mouth of Chi, you can correctly orient the Ba-Gua to your home's floor plan.

The Ba-Gua or Feng Shui Octagon

A foundational Feng Shui concept is the sacred octagon, or Ba-Gua. The Ba-Gua shows you the physical areas where you will perform your Feng Shui cures. By learning the Ba-Gua, you know what parts of your home to adjust to change your life.

The Ba-Gua is a powerful system that comes from the *I Ching,* one of the world's oldest and most profound methods of reading energy patterns. Many branches of Chinese energy theory use the Ba-Gua, including medicine, yoga, martial arts, philosophy, and spirituality. In Feng Shui practice, the Ba-Gua is a tool for understanding the energy patterns of your home or office.

Ba-Gua in Chinese literally means "eight sign" and refers to the octagon pattern shown on the following page. The Ba-Gua system helps you discover which parts of your environment affect which areas of your life. You can use the Ba-Gua to locate nine important sections, or Guas, of your home — eight sides of the octagon, plus the center. Each Gua corresponds to one or more important life areas.

Professor Lin Yun's Feng Shui school uses the Ba-Gua system as its primary tool of reading a home's energy, rather than using a physical compass and literal earth directions (East, West, North, South) as other Feng Shui schools do. The Ba-Gua can be oriented according to the location of your front door, as described on page 26.

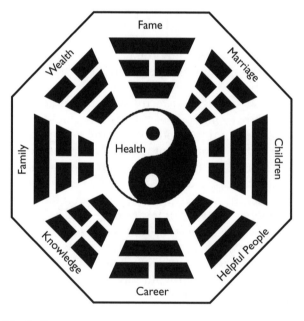

The Ba-Gua

The Nine Sections of the Ba-Gua

The nine sections of the Ba-Gua (eight sides plus the center), with their corresponding house areas and symbolic colors, are:

Ba-Gua Section	House Area	Color
Helpful People	Front right corner	Gray
Career	Front center	Black
Knowledge	Front left corner	Blue
Family	Middle left side	Green/Blue
Wealth	Back left corner	Purple
Fame	Back center	Red
Marriage	Back right corner	Pink
Children	Middle right side	White
Health	Center	Yellow

Though you may feel inclined to favor a particular Gua (such as Wealth) and focus most of your attention on it, all the Guas are important. They all interact with and depend on each other. A weakness in one Gua, like Career, can have unfortunate effects on other Guas and on their areas of life, such as Family, Marriage, and Wealth.

You'll receive more benefit from your Feng Shui when all the Guas of your home and workplace are strong and balanced. If any one section of the Ba-Gua is more important than the others, it is the ninth area: the Center. The Center represents Health and Unity; it supports and feeds all eight sides of the octagon. If you need improvement in many areas of your life at once, or you aren't certain which Gua to work in, you can always do a cure in the Center for overall life benefit.

The Guas and Their Influences

By memorizing the nine sections of the Ba-Gua and their life areas, you can get a quick "energy read" of any home or office you enter. Positions given are in relation to the front wall of the home floor plan. (The front wall is the one that contains the front door.)

▶ **Helpful People Gua.** This Gua affects those who assist you in life: benefactors, friends, and helpers. Also affects travel and relates to the male side of the household: father, brother, son. Located at the *front right corner* of the Ba-Gua.

▶ **Career Gua.** This Gua affects your job, profession, workplace, and connection with the outside world, particularly concerning making a living. Located at the *front center* of the Ba-Gua.

▶ **Knowledge Gua.** This Gua affects self-improvement, wisdom, brightness, mental clarity, intelligence, personal growth, and spirituality. Located at the *front left corner* of the Ba-Gua.

▶ **Family Gua.** This Gua affects your immediate family; also relates to extended family and ancestors. Located at the *middle left side* of the Ba-Gua.

▶ **Wealth Gua.** This Gua affects your money situation and applies to abundance and prosperity in all forms. Located at the *back left corner* of the Ba-Gua.

▶ **Fame Gua.** This Gua affects your reputation and fame; relates to how the community sees you. Also relates to how you see your future and your vision for your life. Located at the *upper center* of the Ba-Gua.

▶ **Marriage Gua.** This Gua affects your primary relationship: husband or wife, boyfriend or girlfriend, significant other. If you have none, affects the likelihood of having one. Also relates to the female side of the household: mother, sister, daughter. Located at the *back right corner* of the Ba-Gua.

▶ **Children Gua.** This Gua affects creative offspring of all kinds: physical children, creative projects, and artistic creativity. Also affects communication. Located at the *middle right side* of the Ba-Gua.

▶ **Health Gua.** This Gua affects physical health; relates to unity and the balance of all things. This important area connects to and unifies the other eight areas. Areas of life that don't fit into a specific Gua can be improved by adjusting the Health Gua. Located in the *center* of the Ba-Gua.

Multiple Levels of the Ba-Gua

You can analyze any space with the Ba-Gua that has a definable Mouth of Chi (main front entrance). The Ba-Gua can be applied to your property, to each floor of your house, and to each room. In this book, we will focus on two important Ba-Guas: the Ba-Gua of the main floor of your house and the Ba-Gua of your bedroom. The Ba-Guas of your office and of your property are also addressed.

Applying the Ba-Gua to Your Home

Applying the Ba-Gua to your home floor plan is one of the most important things you will do in Feng Shui. The Ba-Gua is a basic, necessary Feng Shui method for understanding your home and its energy patterns. After you learn the Ba-Gua, and orient it to your home, you will begin to see where to perform cures to create changes in your life.

To apply the Ba-Gua to your home, overlay the octagon onto your home floor plan. The Ba-Gua's orientation is based on the placement of your front door, rather than on actual Earth directions. "Front door" refers to your main front entrance, never a side, back, or garage door, even if you use one of those doors more often.

Procedure for Placing the Ba-Gua on Your Floor Plan

To place the Ba-Gua on the diagram of your home:

1. Obtain a drawing of your floor plan, best if drawn to scale. If your home has multiple floors, start with the floor containing the front door.
2. Locate the front wall of your house or apartment. The front wall is the wall that contains the front door of your home.
3. Always orient the Ba-Gua so that the Helpful People, Career, and Knowledge Guas are positioned right, center, and left, respectively, along the front wall of the house. (Your front door can be in only one of these three Guas: Helpful People, Career, or Knowledge.)
4. The other five Guas plus the Center of the Ba-Gua are now easy to locate in their respective positions.

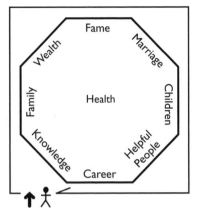

Ba-Gua placed on a house, showing the three possible entrance locations.

Knowledge entrance

Career entrance

Helpful People entrance

Applying the Ba-Gua to Your Bedroom and Yard

You can apply the Ba-Gua to your bedroom and yard according to the steps given on page 26.

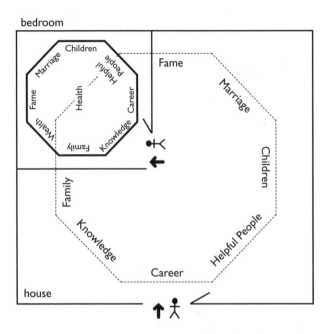

Bedroom Ba-Gua: The door of the room is the Mouth of Chi. In this house, the bedroom is in the Wealth Gua. The entrance of the bedroom is in Knowledge; the house entrance is in Career.

Importance of the Bedroom Ba-Gua

Since the bedroom is "closer" to you than your entire floor plan is, the bedroom Ba-Gua affects you even more powerfully than your house Ba-Gua. This makes it a prime location for performing effective Feng Shui cures.

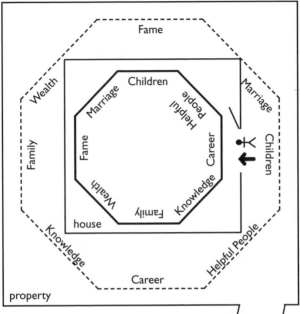

Property Ba-Gua: The Mouth of Chi of the property is the entrance (i.e., the beginning of the driveway at the property line *or* the front walkway at the street if there is no driveway).

Reading Your Ba-Gua

Using the Ba-Gua is as simple as observing the energy characteristics in each Gua of your home's floor plan and relating those characteristics to your life experience.

▸ If an area of your home's octagon has an obvious energy problem, adjusting it will create a direct and sometimes immediate benefit in that life area.

▸ If one of the Guas of your home has no glaring defect but you are still having difficulty in its corresponding life areas, you can improve matters by performing Feng Shui cures in the area, selecting from the appropriate chapters of this book.

Feng Shui Cures

Once you understand the Ba-Gua and apply it to your home, you are ready to learn about Feng Shui cures. Cures are Feng Shui in action.

The term *cure* means any adjustment you make to your home using Feng Shui principles. A Feng Shui cure is any change you make to your space to improve or correct the chi, with a positive intention in mind. Cures are the specific methods by which you can balance the energy flow in your surroundings, creating new and higher levels of energy and well-being. They can be as simple (and as powerful) as cleaning your home or putting fresh flowers on the dining room table, or as major as moving to a brand-new home to invoke major life changes.

Using Minor Additions to Create Major Life Changes

To implement your cures easily and effectively, we will primarily use the Method of Minor Additions to create major life changes. Professor Lin Yun created the Minor Additions Method as a way of energetically "using 4 ounces to move 1,000 pounds." Using this method to add the appropriate Feng Shui items to your home and office will create powerful energy shifts in the environment, which will result in changes you want in your life.

When using Minor Additions cures, adding the right item to the right place with the right intention works wonders for both life enhancement and aesthetic improvement. You can usually do these cures inexpensively and without making structural modifications to your home. To use the Minor Additions, apply the items listed on the following pages to your home to create your cures.

MINOR ADDITIONS	SPECIFIC CURES
Light energy	Lights, mirrors, crystal balls
Sound energy	Bells, wind chimes
Living force, vitality	Plants, flowers, aquariums, fishbowls
Hydraulic energy	Fountains, waterfalls, streams
Mobile objects	Mobiles, windmills, wind socks
Heavy objects	Stones, statues, heavy furniture
Powered objects	Appliances, firecrackers
Color	All colors
Other objects	Bamboo flutes, beaded curtains, others
Fragrance	Incense, aromatherapy, essential oils
Touch	Various
Others	Various

Minor Additions and Their Influences

Light energy. Cures from this group bring bright and light-refracting influences into your home. Lights, of course, add additional light and brightness to the environment, an easy way to increase the chi of an area. Mirrors are one of the most versatile Feng Shui tools, providing a wide variety of possible changes. Depending on the intention with which they are used, mirrors can attract, repel, magnify, uplift, expand, pro-tect, or bless any area. Crystal balls refract, diffuse, reflect, expand, and magnify visible and spiritual light, leading to blessing and expansion.

Sound energy. This group uses bells, wind chimes, gongs, and other sound generators to create awakening, enlivening, stimulating, and protecting energy. Sound cures can also help you call forth a message or response.

Living force. Living force cures use vital, nourishing life energy to enhance, heal, nourish, and uplift the chi of an area. Specific cures include plants, flowers, aquariums, and fishbowls.

Hydraulic energy. The dynamic force of water adds flowing, abundant, and prosperous energy to your home or office through the use of fountains, waterfalls, streams, and other water features.

Mobile objects. Mobile objects can create active and cheerful as well as flowing, smooth, and calming energy. Mobile object cures include mobiles, windmills, wind socks, flags, pinwheels, and whirligigs. These objects "move on their own," symbolizing harmony with the natural order of things. These cures can also bring the uplifting energy of brightness and color to your home.

Heavy objects. Heavy objects add solid, grounding, and stabilizing influences to a situation. This category is good to use for calming areas that may be chaotic or "overenergized." Heavy objects you can add to your home include stones, statues, and heavy furniture.

Powered objects. These objects are powered by specific energy sources, including electricity. Cures in this category include electrical appliances — stereos, computers, TVs, washing machines, and air conditioners — and firecrackers. They typically create active, generating chi. In the case of computers and TVs, their energy can symbolize balance.

Color. Any and all types of colors may be used to create Feng Shui cures. Color is one of the most comprehensive and useful ways to create a better life through Feng Shui. Virtually all things have color. In Feng Shui, each color has significance and can be used for multiple purposes.

Other objects. This category includes many different objects used in Feng Shui for specific purposes, such as bamboo flutes and beaded curtains.

Fragrance. The right scent can uplift the spirit, invoke healing, and set a desired mood for your environment. Methods include incense, aromatherapy, and essential oils. Much research has been conducted and many products are emerging worldwide in this rich area for powerful life change — fragrance is a way to connect directly to the inner spirit.

Touch. This Minor Additions group uses the kinesthetic sense. Energetic results include stimulating, alerting, and health-giving influences. An example is a silk vine wrapped around a stairway banister; touching it as you ascend the stairs can indirectly stimulate creativity and the immune system.

Others. The above categories do not contain all possible Feng Shui cures. The additional known and unknown methods are referred to as "Others."

Five Steps to Simple and Easy Cures

Here's how to start doing Feng Shui cures right away in your home and life:

1. Determine which area of your life you want to improve.

2. Find the chapter that pertains to the life area you want to change. Choose the tip that best suits your needs, budget, and intuition. Locate the part of your home or office in which the cure should be done.

3. Perform the cure in your home.

4. That's it! Enjoy the changes in your life.

5. Do more cures for even more results.

Keys to Performing Effective Cures

When you do your Feng Shui cures, you can greatly enhance their effectiveness by invoking a powerful state of mind as you perform them. Feng Shui cures can and will dramatically affect your mind, body, and emotions in addition to your home's environment and energy. Feng Shui cures are not just mechanical acts that "might" work, but holistic shifts created by a dynamic mix of external action and internal energy, a combination of intention, emotion, and action. Your actions and your intentions are both simultaneously directed toward the same goal: the change you want to create in your life!

The true key to success with your Feng Shui cures lies in focusing energy, attention, and emotion. Your internal state is an important part of the cure and helps impress the energetic changes more deeply into your psyche and energy. If you are distracted or thinking about other things while performing your cures, they will have less power than is possible. If you are fully engaged, with a positive, excited mind-set, and are sincerely focused on the task at hand, your cures will be much more effective. Doing your cures in this way, you will be successfully using both levels of Feng Shui, the visible and the invisible.

The Two Vital Levels of the Cure Process

Professor Lin Yun emphasizes two levels or parts of Feng Shui cures, the visible level and the invisible level. Each level provides an important part of the cure.

1. **The Visible Level.** The visible or external level of the cure concerns the physical environment. The visible level is the external arena where the physical adjustment occurs. The visible level creates just part of the cure's effectiveness. Physical action creates the visible level of the cure. The visible level is where you make an actual change to improve your environment, like placing a wind chime, hanging a mirror, or moving the bed.

2. **The Invisible Level.** This is the internal level of the cure, the arena of your hopes, dreams, and desires. The invisible level is the real power behind the visible side of your reality. Paradoxically, the invisible level of the cure can create a large portion of its effectiveness. The invisible level is where you have a strong desire for what you want (intention) and mentally see it coming true for yourself (visualization).

Visualize Your Cures

Among Feng Shui schools, Professor Lin Yun's Feng Shui is unique in its strong emphasis on the invisible aspects of the cure and the power of using visualization.

Visible + Invisible Levels = Maximum Power

Using the visible and the invisible levels together for your cures results in cures that can be 100 percent effective and even produce greater than hoped for results. Therefore, it is vital that each cure you perform include an action (putting a plant in place), an intention (better physical health), and a visualization of your intention (seeing yourself becoming healthier). If you go around your house putting up lots of mirrors, wind chimes, and plants and don't perform the visualization part of your cures, don't be surprised if the results from your cures are less than stellar.

Tapping into the Power

Intention and visualization work together to create the invisible level of your cure. Using them gives you the power to create the changes you want in your life. Intention is "what you want" and visualization is "seeing it happening."

Intention

A powerful intention contains three elements:

1. Knowing clearly what you want.
2. Possessing a strong desire to have it.
3. Believing that it's yours!

As you practice your Feng Shui, work diligently to strengthen and clarify the intentions you have. With each cure, have a clearer and more powerful intention than you did for the last cure. The more focused and clear your intentions are, the more powerful your cures become.

Visualization

Mental visualization is a major key to the success of your cures. Visualization projects your intention into the world and raises the power of the cure greatly. Visualization is clearly seeing what you want and seeing it occurring in your life.

By clearly visualizing what you want, you adjust your own chi and propel yourself powerfully toward new actions, events, and outcomes in your life. When you visualize, see the details you want surrounding your desired events. Also see and feel the excitement and positive emotion you will experience when you've achieved your desire!

The more clear you are about what you want from your cure (your intention) and the more clearly you mentally see it (visualization), the more likely you are to receive it. This sounds very simple, but it is an important step to your Feng Shui success! If you do a cure with an ambiguous intention — "I want more money" — it is not as powerful as doing the same cure with a specific and clear intention: "I will receive in my right hand $3,500 in the form of a cashier's check made out to me, on the 15th of next month" — and clearly visualizing the details surrounding this event.

Three Secrets for Successful Cures

As powerful and vital as visualization is for Feng Shui success, it is just one of the important Three Secrets Professor Lin Yun teaches for reinforcing and strengthening your cures. For greater benefit, learn and use all Three Secrets (see chapter 12).

To help you get started with visualization, suggested visualizations are given along with each cure in upcoming chapters. These suggestions are provided only to help get the ball rolling. If you think of a more powerful and appropriate one for your cure, please use it.

Important Tips to Use with Your Feng Shui Cures

1. Be fully involved. The more involved you are, the more powerful and real your cures become.
2. For maximum effectiveness, pay careful attention to each part of your cures as you do them.
3. Desire is a key factor. The more you want it, the more likely it is to happen.
4. Sincerity — the belief that your cure will be effective — works wonders.
5. Positive emotion is the wellspring of energy for personal life change.
6. Visualization is a key to Feng Shui power. See your goals, wishes, and desires definitely occurring with each cure that you do. This dramatically increases the likelihood that your desires will come true.

Wherever you are right now in your ability and capacity with Feng Shui is fine. If you aren't quite ready to fully believe in Feng Shui or that your cures will definitely work, Feng Shui still has much to offer you. Just jump in, give it your best, and watch your results improve over time.

If the visualizations you do are less than perfect, that's okay. Don't feel any performance pressure about the internal part of Feng Shui. You can do it. Feel satisfied with what you are doing now and use it as a stepping-stone for more success in the future. Your ability will only improve as you go, and so will your Feng Shui cures.

Expecting and Getting Results

Everyone has different results from Feng Shui cures. Some people receive immediate results, while others see their lives gradually improve over time. Still others see no results for a while, then suddenly their lives shift and they see many improvements in a short period of time.

Many times Feng Shui benefits come from unexpected but positive sources. It is difficult to predict exactly how and where changes will occur in a specific life. The best attitude toward results is to have an open, positive expectation, and not be too attached to exactly how or when your results will occur. Also be willing to allow internal changes to take place in your psychology, emotions, and personality. For many people, these inner changes are an important counterpart that occurs along with the "outer" life results.

Maximize Your Cures

Tips on the best ways to use some of the cures can be found on the pages listed below. Please refer to these notes to get the most out of your cures.

Fountains	Page 42
Mirrors	Page 50
Crystal balls	Page 52
Red ribbons	Page 53
Lighting	Page 71
Bamboo flutes	Page 72
Plants	Page 79
Wind chimes	Page 47

— 2 —
Wealth

THE WEALTH AREA OF LIFE is highly important to almost everyone and a prime area for Feng Shui cures. True wealth is the energetic experience of abundance. Wealth enables and strengthens many other areas of life. It allows us to help others, as well as deservedly enjoying the better things in life. The Wealth Gua of the Ba-Gua relates specifically to money, but also refers to prosperity and abundance in all areas of life.

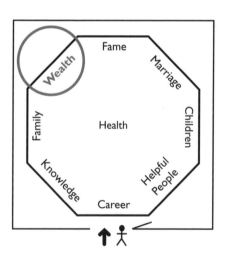

The Wealth Gua

Method I: Increase Flowing Water in Your Life

Water is a universal symbol of wealth and prosperity. The image of a rich harvest from the sea or living near a fruitful river has always meant being blessed with the wealth of nature. Water's meaning is strongly connected to the Chinese culture and the art of Feng Shui.

According to Professor Lin Yun's energy theory, water's influence can be divided into two energy states: moving water (flowing, active, and circulating) and still water (contained bodies of water). Both are connected to wealth, although in different ways.

Moving Water. In its mobile or active state, water represents the flow of money as well as having connections to many people, all of whom may help you. Therefore, having flowing water in your space helps you have a strongly circulating cash flow and a healthy network of contacts and associates.

Still Water. Still water features, such as ponds, lakes, or swimming pools on your property, symbolize stored, accumulated wealth. If these still bodies of water are clear, they symbolize a clear, calm state of mind and a clean financial picture; if cloudy or turbulent, they create mental turmoil and a less healthy financial picture.

Of the two types of water, moving water is the more powerful prosperity generator, because moving water carries with it the dynamic energy for creating additional wealth. Applying a still water cure to your environment, however, such as a swimming pool in the back yard, can also be a powerful wealth cure.

⊕ *Attract wealth with a fountain in front of your house.*

Placing a fountain in front of your home is an excellent way to attract flowing money energy and help conduct it into your home. This fountain can be located anywhere in your front yard or closer to the front door. Since moving water near the main entrance to the home is positive for wealth, this is a particularly good place to locate your exterior fountain, as long as it doesn't block the path into the house. When doing this cure, visualize that wealth is now flowing into your life.

⊕ *Generate money with a fountain in the Wealth area.*

By applying the Ba-Gua (see chapter 1) to your home floor plan, you'll be able to determine the Wealth Guas of your environment, located in the far left corner of your office, house, and bedroom. Since the chi that circulates in your Wealth Guas is a major contributor to your personal wealth situation, placing moving water in one or more of your Wealth Guas is an easy and

---

Fountain Notes

When placing an exterior fountain in front of the house, it is important that the flow of water, if not flowing straight up, be toward the front door, not away from the house. The latter direction could cause wealth to leave the household. It is not necessary to keep your fountain running all the time in order for it to be an effective Feng Shui cure. But keep it in good working condition at all times so as not to symbolize a stoppage of money flow to you. If you have an existing fountain in disrepair, fixing it at once would be a priority for your wealth situation.

powerful wealth cure. When you put this cure in place, reinforce it by visualizing that wealth is now flowing to you abundantly.

Although larger is generally better, fountains of any size can be effective, according to your spatial and aesthetic requirements. Fountains can be obtained at nurseries, landscaping outlets, and other stores. You can also easily and inexpensively create your own fountain with a ceramic container, some smooth rocks, and a small aquarium water pump.

⊕ *Stimulate wealth chi by adding an aquarium.*

Aquariums and fishbowls are other prime wealth cures for both home and office environments. You may have noticed the large, beautiful aquariums located in many Chinese restaurants and banks. They're not there by accident: Such strong wealth generators are placed to create powerful wealth chi for the owners of these businesses. Aquariums add wealth energy and the fertility-giving dimension of living fish to the power of moving water, resulting in an abundantly symbolic and effective wealth cure. Prime locations to place an aquarium are: near the entrance or in the entryway, in the Career Gua of the house, and in the Wealth Gua of the house. As always, remember to visualize prosperity and abundance in your life to make this cure more effective.

⊕ *Add power to your aquariums with auspicious numbers and colors.*

Professor Lin Yun's teachings contain further ways to enhance the wealth-creating power of your aquariums using color and number symbology. A strong number of fish to have is 9, or a multiple of 9 (18, 27, etc.). Nine is a very powerful number, representing culmination and completion. The color aspect of your fish can be enhanced by using eight red fish (not orange) and one black one for each set of nine. Red and black are powerful Feng Shui colors; red signifies power, healing and wealth, while black represents money, authority, and wisdom. As you perform this cure, visualize that the energy of the aquarium is enhancing your wealth. As you visualize enhanced wealth, see in detail the ways you will use and enjoy the funds that come your way.

Replace any fish that don't survive as soon as possible, keeping the number to a multiple of 9. Feng Shui lore says that if one of your fish dies, it has absorbed negative chi or bad luck meant for the owner of the aquarium — a good reason to replace it immediately.

✸ Supercharge your aquarium with gold coins.

Sprinkle nine gold coins on the gravel bed of your aquarium, visualizing that your wealth is continuously increasing and is like the ocean itself. Use real or fake gold coins for this cure; the best number of coins to use is a multiple of 9. Twenty-seven is a particularly powerful number, as it contains three sets of 9. When placing these coins, visualize your personal "gold" and wealth building daily.

✸ Increase abundance with a picture of "fishermen bringing in full nets."

The ocean is a universal representation of prosperity. Since ancient times, a bountiful harvest from the sea meant that society would experience plenty in the months ahead. A great way to tap into this symbolic energy is to place a photo or painting of fishermen hauling in full nets from the sea near your entrance, or in any Wealth Gua in your home. The appropriate image for your home may require searching to find, but is worth the time and energy as you enjoy your increased prosperity. For greatest effect with this cure, visualize enjoying an abundant life.

⊕ *Enhance your flow of money with a picture of a waterfall.*

Place a large photo or poster of a vigorous waterfall near the entrance of the house. When you hang this picture in place, visualize abundant money pouring continuously and easily into your life, like endlessly flowing water.

⊕ *Stop wealth outflow by stopping the leaking water.*

Water problems can lead to the loss of wealth. Any leaking, dripping, or seeping water in your environment can represent hemorrhaging in your home or business financial picture. The cure is simple: Fix all your leaks immediately, while visualizing that expenditures are now under control and not leaking in known or unknown ways.

This cure includes any and all household leaks: faucets, sinks, pipes, appliances, roof, basement, and outdoor fixtures. Generally, the closer the leak is to you, the more impact it has. (See The Theory of Relative Positioning, page 19.)

Business and Leaking Water

This cure bears consideration if your business is experiencing a mysterious "leakage of funds." Ruthlessly hunt down any leaks and apply all measures necessary to see them fully fixed. A leak near the entrance, in a Wealth Gua, or in the center of an office or home can be especially harmful to your wealth.

✦ *Stimulate the motion of prosperity with a fish mobile.*

Mobiles bring circulating, flowing energy into your home. To combine the mobile's energy with "fish power," add a fish mobile to your home, either near the entrance (inside or outside) or in the Wealth Gua of your house. Hang your mobile from a red ribbon (cut to a multiple of 9" long). When you place this cure, visualize increased prosperity in your life.

Method II: Enhance Your Wealth Guas

The Wealth Gua of the Ba-Gua relates to money, but also refers to prosperity and abundance in all areas of life.

✦ *Awaken your wealth with a wind chime.*

Place a nice-sounding metal wind chime (preferably brass) in the Wealth corner of your home. The chi in your Wealth Gua can be "awakened" and enlivened by using a wind chime as a cure. Wind chimes are noted for their activating, generating, and protective qualities. Chimes can also symbolically call forth a message, such as a request for additional funds. Chimes are most effective if hung with a 9" red cord or ribbon.

When you hang your wind chime, visualize that "wealth forces," both known and unknown, are awakening and working on your behalf. You can further activate this cure by ringing your wealth chime at regular intervals or whenever you choose.

✦ *Magnify wealth with a mirror in the bedroom.*

The bedroom is another powerful environment for enhancing your wealth energy. Place a mirror in the Wealth Gua of the room to enhance your wealth (from the doorway, wealth is in the back left corner). See money being drawn to you like a magnet through the power of the mirror. Visualize your life bcoming more enjoyable with your newly increased wealth.

⊛ *Build on your money — keep it in a Wealth Gua.*

A great symbolic way to align yourself to greater prosperity is to stash a bank savings book (from an active account) in the Wealth Gua of your home or bedroom tucked inside a red envelope. This cure will be empowered by visualizing the size of the book and the dollar amounts inside it growing steadily.

A variation of this cure is to keep actual gold pieces (9 is a good amount) hidden in the Wealth Gua of your choice. As you place this cure, visualize your pile of gold building. Another way to do this cure is to use nine brand-new $1 bills or even 27 shiny new pennies as "seed money" stored in your wealth corner.

⊕ *Stabilize your financial condition
   using stones.*

If your money situation is chaotic or
ungrounded, depth and peace can be created by
putting a heavy object in the wealth corner of
your home or yard. Heavy items, such as large
stones and statues, added to the Wealth Gua will
bring grounding and stabilizing forces to your
money situation. A large potted plant can also
create a grounding and balancing effect in this
location. As you put this cure in place, it is
helpful to visualize yourself experiencing greatly increased financial calmness. See a smooth,
orderly condition, with plenty of actual income
and your bills being paid on time.

Be sure to use a sense of balance when choosing the items for this cure. If your wealth life is
in upheaval, it probably won't be highly effective to place a 1"-diameter pebble in the money
corner. On the other hand, be sure not to put
such a huge object in an inside wealth corner
that it blocks or stagnates your wealth energy.

Note: When using stones and rocks as wealth
cures, those with smooth edges are recommended over those with sharp, jagged edges, which
can symbolically "cut" your money.

Mix-and-Match Cures
to Maximize Your Wealth

The wealth corner cures given here can be combined for greater effect. Feel free to perform multiple cures using these ideas, visualizing what you
want with each cure you do.

Method III: Protect and Strengthen the Stove and Cook

Feng Shui teaches that health and wealth are intimately connected. Indeed, health is said to be the foundation and springboard for wealth. Your stove is of major importance to your personal wealth scenario. The stove is the specific wealth generator of the home. Its condition, placement, and overall ambience are major contributing factors to the health of everyone in the household. (*Note:* The Feng Shui stove cures and principles apply to your life whether you cook most meals at home or typically eat out in restaurants.)

⊕ *Protect and empower the cook with a mirror behind the stove.*

An important guideline for wealth creation is to make sure the cook is "protected" while he or she stands at the stove. It is important for your wealth that the cook not be startled while cooking, even in a subtle way. If the cook does become startled, even unconsciously, the chi of the food will be upset, leading to health and wealth problems, unexpected accidents, and possible illnesses in the home.

Most stoves, except those on kitchen "islands," are placed so that the cooks will have their backs to the kitchen door, not allowing them to see who is approaching.

A basic and powerful stove cure is to place a mirror on the wall behind your stove. This mirror enables cooks to see easily who is approaching from behind, creating a sense of safety and protection. This feeling translates into more wealth for you on many levels.

Mirror behind stove, with optional mirror strip behind the burners.

Mirror Notes

It is important that all mirrors used for Feng Shui (and ideally all mirrors in your home) be crystal clear, clean, and distortion-free. Mirrors represent the mind and influence our self-image, reflecting back to us who and what we are. Imperfections in your mirrors can cause problems in these important areas. The larger the mirror, the better. Good shapes are octagonal, round, square, and rectangular. Mirrors should also be free of chips, cracks, smokiness, glazing, and etchings. It is recommended to avoid mirror arrangements that have multiple pieces, although a small beveled edge is generally acceptable. When hanging mirrors, ensure that they are high enough so they don't "cut off the head" of any (adult) household occupants.

For maximum results with this cure, visualize your increased wealth and prosperity.

The "mirror behind the stove" concept can also be used to perform a second wealth cure. This cure is done by making sure that the mirror behind the stove extends down far enough to reflect the burners. By reflecting your burners with the mirror, you symbolically double the number of burners, which generates more wealth. This doubling effect is a booster of money energy for the household. Visualize, when you place this mirror, that your wealth is being increased.

If you want to perform the "mirror doubling the burners" cure, but the construction of your stove prevents a mirror on the wall from extending down far enough to see the burners, you can custom-cut a small rectangular mirror strip that fits directly above the burners and reflects them. (See illustration on opposite page.)

⊕ *Up your wealth power by using all your stove burners.*

If the stove is the home's wealth-creating appliance, the burners themselves are its specific money generators. If you use some of your stove burners more heavily than others, your unused burners are "dormant," which can put a damper on your creation of money. Start using all your burners equally to ensure that your stove is providing you with maximum earning power. Visualize that maximum earning power is yours and increased wealth is coming your way.

⊕ *Increase your money power by tuning up your stove.*

A stove burner that doesn't work at all is an even greater impediment to your income. It is very important that all parts of your stove be in good working order, including all burners, lights, knobs, and switches. The money cure to perform here is to make your stove repairs as quickly as possible, and to visualize smooth, unimpeded wealth being generated from now on.

⊕ *Protect the cook with a chime or crystal.*

Another powerful cook protection cure is to hang a wind chime from the ceiling directly over where the cook stands at the stove. This cure helps keep unwelcome energy away from the cooking location and can also cause positive money energy to flow to you.

An alternate technique is to hang a crystal ball over the cook, rather than a chime (see box below). As you place your crystal, visualize

---

Types of Crystals

The type of crystals for Feng Shui are specifically round (spherical), faceted, prismatic, leaded-glass crystal balls (not plain glass balls or mineral crystals from the earth). The spherical factor is important because they can handle energy coming from any direction. The facets allow the balls to refract light and emit rays, contributing to the light's expansive nature. The crystals come in 10- to 70-mm diameters. Larger crystals are more effective than smaller. Crystals 40 mm or larger are recommended for the cures in this book.

Faceted, leaded-glass crystal

---

expansiveness, brightness, and protection being added to your wealth picture.

✧ *Increase money energy by keeping the stove clean.*

The cleanliness of the stove has a direct connection to your wealth situation. Keeping the stove clean ensures fresh wealth energy in your life. Food and cooking are intimately tied to your health and wealth. A dirty stove stagnates the flow of wealth and makes it harder to make and keep money. An unclean stove can contribute to financial entanglements and assorted money problems.

Move your stove out from the wall and give the entire stove a thorough cleaning from top to bottom, including behind and under the stove. You may be amazed at what you'll find — your wealth will improve and your entire house will feel cleaner and more comfortable. Keeping the stove cleaner on a regular basis is a powerful Feng Shui practice. As you clean, be sure to visualize that you are now cleaning away any money problems and opening up the energy for more wealth to come to you.

The Importance of Red Ribbons

Cures that are hung, including crystals, chimes, bells, and mobiles, are always hung using a red ribbon, string, or cord. The ribbon used is cut to a multiple of 9" or 9 cm (9, 18, 27, etc.) in length. This doesn't mean that the chime or crystal ball itself must hang down from the ceiling in an exact multiple of 9". You may hang it as far down as is aesthetically appropriate for you; it is the hanging medium itself that is to be cut to a multiple of 9. Extra ribbon can be tied at the top, if you wish.

✦ *Eliminate confusion and bad luck by adjusting "door-to-stove" pathways.*

If your stove sits in a "pass-through" kitchen, with a pathway between two doors crossing in front of the stove, ill fortune can be close at hand. A pass-through situation strips healthy chi away from the stove and negatively affects many areas of life, including wealth, health, marriage, and family harmony. It is more favorable to have the stove in a more protected, but not cramped, location.

Cures for the "stove in the pathway" condition include placing a crystal, chime, or bell in front of each doorway to disperse inflowing chi, and hanging a wind chime over the cook's head, or you can use both cures. Use a red ribbon (9" or multiples of 9 in length) to hang your cure. Powerfully visualize peace, wealth, and general good fortune as you perform this important cure.

✦ *Increase your wealth by removing obstructing hoods and ovens.*

A hood or microwave oven at or below the cook's head level or an oven over the stovetop can substantially "compress" the chi around your stove, decreasing the vitality and strength of both the food and your wealth energy. This inauspicious condition can be improved by several methods:

▸ Place a mirror behind the stove to help expand the stove and compensate for the compressing energy. (See cure on page 49.)
▸ Remove the offending unit, replacing it with another, higher fan if needed.
▸ If removal is not feasible, hang a crystal ball from a red ribbon within the hood where you

can see it, but not hanging down too far. This cure can brighten the picture and nicely nullify repressive energy. Visualize when doing these cures that your wealth and income are increasing on a continuous basis.

⊕ *Attract fresh, lively money chi with healthy plants in your kitchen.*

The place for preparing the food should always be lively, vital, and full of energy. Bringing three healthy new plants into your kitchen will bring in fresh chi, which will enhance both your wealth and your health. Plants also symbolically "feed the fire" of the stove, increasing its strength and brightness. When performing this cure, mentally visualize your growing and glowing prosperity.

⊕ *Promote health by keeping the kitchen bright and light.*

An excellent way to brighten the money picture of your life is to increase the lighting level in your kitchen, an important wealth-generating room. It is amazing how many kitchens are dark, depressing rooms, with dim or even fluorescent lighting. Food preparation and cooking in such an environment are detrimental to wealth creation and to your health. The solution is clear: Install bright and pleasant lighting in your kitchen.

To remedy this problem, you can either install a brighter main light in the kitchen or add more lamps on your countertops. These lights do not need to be on every time you're in the kitchen to be effective cures, although they should be in good working order.

✦ *Let your ship finally come in with a boat-shaped bowl in your kitchen.*

Another easy wealth cure for the kitchen is to add a boat-shaped bowl filled with fruit. Fill your boat with 9 or 27 pieces of tasty-looking artificial fruit, or regularly put in fresh fruit. This arrangement symbolizes plenty and abundance. Visualize a fruitful harvest of income as you install this cure in your kitchen.

Method IV: Use "Money Colors" to Stimulate Wealth

✦ *Empower your life with a red front door.*

The front door is one of the most important points in your home, symbolizing the entrance of energy. If the entrance is auspicious (lucky, wealthy), it bodes well for your wealth. The color of your door has a strong impact on your thoughts, personal energy, and overall money situation.

Red is the most auspicious and powerful color in Feng Shui. Painting your front door red (the brighter, the better) is a classic wealth cure and overall life-improvement method. Visualize that positive events and opportunities are coming your way.

✦ *Decorate your life using wealth colors.*

Wealth colors for walls include green, red, blue, and purple. Avoid making a room too dark, which can be depressing. You can paint only one wall of a room a wealth color. Visualize that you are receiving and having more income and wealth when you do this cure.

⊕ *Wear wealth colors for a prosperous future.*

The colors of your wardrobe are another powerful area you can use for creating wealth. **Red** carries with it wealth, power, luck, and healing energies. **Purple** is the strongest wealth color, representing royalty and an "excess" of the luckiness of red. **Green** is a strong wealth color, symbolizing money, new beginnings, growth, and health. **Blue** stands for royalty, knowledge, and wealth.

When you wear wealth colors, be sure to visualize your goals and desires coming true in detail.

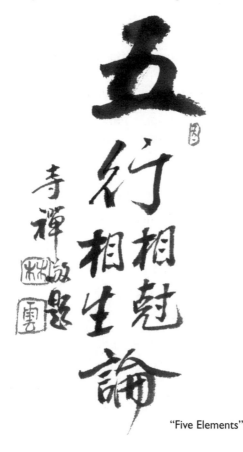

"Five Elements"

3

Love and Romance

YOU CAN ADD CURES for the universally important life area of love and romance, relationship and marriage. Cures you find here will help you improve (or attract) your primary relationship — the relationship with your lover or partner. (In this chapter, the terms "marriage" and "relationship" are interchangeable and refer to "love" and "romance" as well.)

Parts of your home most connected with the life area of marriage are:

- Your bed.
- Your bedroom as a whole.
- The Marriage Gua of your bedroom's Ba-Gua.
- The Marriage Gua of your home's Ba-Gua.

Since the bed and bedroom are also primary symbols of "Self" (you), many cures in this chapter are powerful for changing your entire life, as well as your relationship.

Qualities of the heart, open communication, and truthfulness are paramount for success in this life area. To strengthen an existing relationship, it is very beneficial to create nurturing, warm, and healthy energy in the above parts of your home. To attract a new relationship, "generating" and "activating" chi is helpful. Also, because marriage is a highly

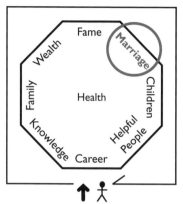

Marriage Gua of home and bedroom

home-oriented phenomenon, it can benefit from Feng Shui cures done in almost any part of the house.

Method I: Locate Your Bedroom Powerfully

According to Feng Shui Master Professor Lin Yun, the bedroom is a highly important room of your house, if not the most important. You spend a third of your life in this room. It's your prime environment for rest, relaxation, and rejuvenation. The bedroom is the room most connected to relationship and marriage in your life. The master bedroom should be the most private and secluded room in the house — a place where you feel very comfortable, safe, and protected enough to "let your guard down" for a few hours.

Situating the master bedroom in the right location within your house is a powerful Feng Shui cure that creates many benefits in relationships, wealth, health, and other life areas. The bedroom ideally should be in one of your home's two "power spots," which are located in the Wealth Gua and the Marriage Gua. These are the two strongest points in most homes, being farthest from the door. If your bedroom is in a poor Feng Shui position, the ideal solution is to move your bedroom to the strongest location in the house. If no room in your house is good for a bedroom location, perform as many cures within the bedroom as possible, with the long-term aim of finding a home that has good bedroom Feng Shui.

According to the Theory of Relative Positioning, the bedroom is the closest room to yourself (body), making it the most important room in your life. When looking for a home, if you find a house that seems great but the master bedroom is inauspicious, this alone can be a Feng Shui reason to reject the house.

✦ *Choose a bedroom location as far back from the front door as possible.*

The farther from the front door the bedroom is, the more you will feel in control of your home and life. This principle and those that follow are not requirements, but ideal conditions to aim for. The more of these principles your bedroom is aligned with, the more supported your life and relationships will be. When conforming to these principles, visualize that your relationship and love life are improving easily and dramatically.

✦ *Choose a bedroom behind the "midline" of the house.*

For household peace, auspicious wealth, and a strong marriage, the master bedroom should be behind the "midline" of the house. This is a quieter, more powerful place than the part of

> ## Bedroom Location
>
> Locating the bedroom in one of your home's two "power spots" creates a stronger base for your relationship to grow. When choosing a location, keep in mind these principles:
>
> ▸ The bedroom entrance should not be hidden or difficult to get to.
> ▸ The bedroom should not be in an area of the house that feels blocked (no circulation or movement) or stagnant (depressing or stuffy).
> ▸ The master bedroom should be the largest bedroom in the house.

the house in front of the midline, which is more concerned with activity and social life.

If the bedroom is in front of the midline of the house, rest can be disturbed and marriage chi affected. The situation is even worse if the master bedroom is in front of the Mouth of Chi (main front door). This unfortunate arrangement can lead to one partner being gone from home often, marriage difficulty, or even the relationship splitting apart.

⊕ *Empower your relationship by moving your bedroom.*

First, if you have a room farther back in your house that will work as a master bedroom, you can move your bedroom into that room. Visualize your marriage or primary relationship blossoming there.

Another option is to place a mirror in the back part of the house that is in line with your bed. The job of this mirror will be to symbolically "pull" your bed and bedroom into a more power-ful location in the back of the house, without physically moving it. This cure will strongly increase the Feng Shui energy of your bed. Place a sizable mirror at torso height, so that it can reflect your head.

⊕ *Remedy a hidden, blocked, or stagnant bed-room entrance with crystals or chimes.*

This type of bedroom can cause many road-blocks in life. The situation can be cured by hanging a 50 mm or larger crystal ball or a pleasant-sounding metal wind chime directly outside the bedroom door from a red ribbon. Visualize with this cure that the path to your room is lively and energetic, your life is smooth and open, and your marriage is being recharged.

Situations to Avoid

▶ Ideally, the bedroom should not be over a garage. This placement can lead to chaotic, disruptive energy coming up into the room from cars enter-ing the garage. To cure this situation, hang a crystal ball from a red ribbon in the garage over each car.

▶ The bedroom should not be near an active street or have a street or driveway pointed directly at it. This includes bedrooms adjacent to an attached garage, where the car is pointed directly at the room. If the room is near street activity, restless-ness, impatience, and irritation can result. If cars point directly at the room, physical accidents may befall the occupants. To cure this, use the Ba-Gua mirror solution given for noisy bedrooms (page 63).

⊕ *Use chimes or crystals to cure a too small bedroom.*

As with the cure above, hang a crystal or wind chime in the center of the bedroom to create an expansion of the chi. Be certain to picture your space and marriage expanding and growing.

⊕ *Cure a noisy or disturbed bedroom with mirrors.*

Place a Ba-Gua mirror on the outside wall of your bedroom facing the oncoming vehicles or the neighbors' house (see the Ba-Gua mirror cure on page 146). Visualize yourself being strongly protected and empowered by this mirror. Also see your relationship now strongly enhanced.

Method II: Place Your Bed in the "Commanding Position"

The "Commanding Position" is the most fortunate and lucky position for bed placement. The Commanding Position concept is based on these five principles:

1. The relative position of the bed to the door of the bedroom (or Mouth of Chi) is more important than the earth direction (east, south, west, north) that the bed faces. Since the Mouth of Chi is the main entry point of energy for the room, how the bed relates to it is a key factor for life.

2. The position of the bed should permit the widest possible scope of vision for the viewer — the more of the room you can see, the more ease, expansion, and control you will feel.

3. The door (Mouth of Chi) should be seen easily from the bed, providing a feeling of peace and safety.

4. The bed should not face the Mouth of Chi directly. If it does, accidents or health issues can result. Keeping the bed out of the direct pathway of the bedroom door is important for keeping "out of harm's way."

5. The head of the bed should be against a wall or against a corner, as in the illustrations below.

Following these five principles will create a powerful and balanced position. Since bed position is one of the most important Feng Shui factors in life, placing your bed in the Commanding Position is a very significant and powerful cure for your relationship, health, wealth, and many other areas of your life.

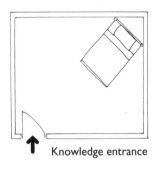

Knowledge entrance

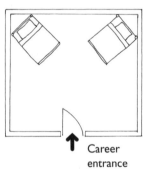

Career entrance

Commanding position for bed placement. Career entrance has two options for best bed placement.

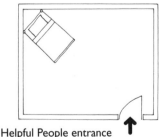

Helpful People entrance

✤ *Improve your relationship with powerful bed placement.*

The corners of the room farthest from the door are the two most powerful spots in the room and are prime locations for bed placement (see above illustration). The farther your bed is from the door, the more space in the room you command and the more empowered you feel. You should have the widest view possible of the interior of the room. This bed position builds self-esteem and gives you a solid foundation for life and for your relationship. Visualize this result in your life as you place your bed.

✤ *Enjoy a better life and relationship by seeing the door from the bed.*

It is very important that you are able to see the door easily while lying on your back in your bed. Seeing the door lets you know what circumstances and relationships are coming toward you and gives a strong feeling of reassurance and safety. Not being able to see the door from the bed can lead to fear, doubts, and feelings of insecurity.

If it's not feasible to place your bed so you can see the door, the suggested cure is to place a mirror on the opposite wall, so you can see the door in the mirror. With this cure, visualize being in charge of your life and enjoying a great relationship.

✤ *Keep the head of your bed against a wall.*

Having the head of your bed "freestanding" (not up against a wall) is a good recipe for mental turmoil and relationship stress. This position can also cause insomnia and bad dreams. (The exception to this rule is if the bed is in a corner at a 45° angle, which is a very good bed position.)

It can also cause insomnia to have the head of your bed against a window. This position can make you feel unsafe and unsure of things in your life. It can also cause physical and mental health problems because of energy flows that are running across the bed — and you — and out the window. Having the head of your bed against a solid wall that has only a small, high window above the bed is usually fine.

A suggested visualization for this cure is to see yourself and your relationship being safe and on a very solid foundation.

⊕ *Solidify your relationship with a proper headboard and footboard.*

For additional relationship and life support, your bed should feature a strong and solid headboard. A bed that has a good headboard has better support for your relationship than the same bed with no headboard. It is very beneficial to fix or replace a headboard that wobbles or is made of bars or slats. A loose headboard can create insecurity in your life, while one made of bars can give you a subconscious "imprisoned" feeling. Also, make sure the footboard does not extend above the mattress. If it does, your progress and career can be hampered.

When performing either of these cures, visualize a stronger, more balanced life and relationship.

Method III: Improve the Chi of Your Bed

⊕ *Get a new life with a brand-new bed.*

A great way to get a new start in life, as well as in your relationship, is to get a brand-new bed. A new bed is a powerful symbol of fresh

Secondhand Beds

It is highly recommended to avoid getting a used bed, including a hand-me-down or gift. Used beds carry with them the chi from previous owners, which can affect your chi. They will never have the freshness that a new bed does. The best energy comes from being the first person ever to have slept on the bed. To create fresh, new chi in your current bed, a good substitute cure is to get new sheets and pillowcases. When you have performed this cure, visualize having a fresh, new relationship life.

opportunities for the inner and outer realms of your life. Aim for the best bed you can afford and you will see great benefit. An especially powerful time to apply this cure is when moving into a new home or when a major relationship has ended.

🌐 *Place a chime or bell over the bed to awaken your relationship energy.*

The space over the bed is a prime location for powerful Feng Shui cures. Placing a wind chime or brass bell over your bed can bring in refreshing new energy to your love life. Think of it as a metaphorical "wake-up call" for your bed and your own energy. A chime or bell will serve nicely to stimulate love and new activity in the romance sector of your life. For full results from this cure, visualize the beginning of something new and wonderful in your relationship.

🌐 *Expand your relationship by hanging a crystal ball.*

According to Professor Lin Yun, the closer a part of the environment is to you (your body), the more effect it has on your life. Next to your body, the closest Feng Shui environment is your bed.

In addition to correct placement and orientation of the bed itself, the space surrounding the bed is a powerful arena for Feng Shui cures. An excellent cure to positively impact your relationship, as well as health, mental clarity, and activating your personal energy, is to hang a crystal ball (from a red ribbon) over the head of your bed. The expansive, bright, and reflective qualities of the crystal ball will expand your wisdom, bring new light into your relationship, and help clear away disagreements and problems.

✦ *Add love to your love life with pink sheets or blankets.*

To increase love in an existing relationship or to bring in a new romance, put pink sheets on your bed. Pink is the primary Feng Shui color for love. Having this influence next to the body is an easy way to adjust your chi and empower the relationship area of your life. When placing pink sheets on your bed, mentally see an expansion of love spontaneously occurring in your life.

Mirrors across from the Bed

In traditional Feng Shui a mirror located across from the foot of the bed is not recommended. It is believed that this mirror can create insomnia, negative dreams, and startle one upon awakening.

In Professor Lin Yun's Feng Shui, a mirror hung across from the foot of the bed creates positive benefits. These include a stronger sense of self-esteem, better recall of dreams, more awareness about yourself, and increased ability to move forward in life.

✥ *Unify your relationship by fixing your king-size bed.*

King-size beds are a special case because their box springs come in two pieces, creating a hidden split in the bottom layer of the bed. This contributes a divisive influence to your relationship and it is especially negative because it occurs on a hidden level.

There are a couple of ways to remedy this situation and create more unity. You can get a new queen-size bed or you can simply use the healing energy of the color red to mend the split. Place a red king-size sheet over the box spring (between the mattress and box spring sections of the bed) and visualize the two box spring sections fused into one and your relationship being solid, happy, and unified on all levels.

✥ *Enjoy a better relationship by removing subconscious blocks.*

Keeping things stored under your bed is a sure recipe for hidden obstacles in your relationship life. If this space is blocked, you can be blocked in relationship and other areas of your life on unseen levels. Clearing out anything stored under your bed has a significant relieving and releasing effect on your relationship. For greatest effect, visualize old and stuck problems clearing away and abundant new freedom and energy coming into your life and your relationship.

Enhancing Chi

If you want to strengthen your own chi, hang a crystal directly over where your head rests when you sleep. To enhance the chi of both partners, hang it above and midway between where your heads rest.

Method IV: Cures for Your Bedroom and for Your Marriage Guas

⊕ *Create harmony and unity by adding a round mirror to the bedroom.*

The energy of a mirror can attract and expand relationship energy; round shapes symbolize unity and harmony. A round mirror in your bedroom is a way to attract a new relationship or add harmony and unity to your existing one. This cure is more powerful if you place the mirror in the Marriage Gua of the bedroom. Strengthen the mirror by making it a multiple of 9" in diameter. Visualize that your relationship is now more peaceful, harmonious, and strengthened.

⊕ *Save your energy — protect your bed from a bathroom door.*

Many houses are now being built with master bedroom suites, incorporating a bathroom and dressing room into the master bedroom. While this is a convenient arrangement, it can also create Feng Shui problems. A bathroom door near your bed can cause a major drain on relationship and other life areas. The best course is to keep your bed as far away from a bathroom door as possible. The foot of the bed should not point directly at a bathroom door, as this position can lead to health problems.

It is better to close bathroom doors located inside bedrooms. This prevents relationship and health chi from leaking into the bathroom, causing a drain on your life energy. Put a full-length mirror on the outside of a bathroom door within a bedroom. This helps keep the bedroom's energy more contained and coherent.

Visualize your energy being retained, your life growing, and your relationship improving.

⊕ *Bring in new, fresh chi by adding fresh flowers.*

Bringing freshly cut flowers into the bedroom brings fresh energy into your relationship. Flowers also add good luck to your life. Change the flowers as soon as they start to wane.

Also, remove all dead or dried flowers from the bedroom and the rest of the house. These symbols of past, "used-up" energy do not help attract a lively and vivacious mate. Avoid dried (dead) flowers; they can have a negative impact on the environment and the people within it.

When you perform this cure, visualize that you are clearing the past and are free from anything that was holding you back.

⊕ *Brighten your relationship with a stronger bedroom light.*

Another strong cure for relationships is to place a bright light in the bedroom. The main light in the bedroom should be strong enough to light the room well on its own. Bright chi in this room leads to a positive, bright future for you and your mate. This cure works whether or not you turn on the bright light — its presence is enough. The light must be in good working condition. This cure is also good for health and for strong personal chi. Visualize a brighter future for yourself and your marriage or relationship.

Lighting

The best light for good Feng Shui is strong and bright, not harsh, glaring, or overpowering, especially in an overhead light.

Bamboo Flute Notes

Bamboo flutes used in cures symbolize and provide the following beneficial qualities:

▶ Peace, safety, protection, and strength, symbolized by bamboo.

▶ Life improving in stages. Each section of bamboo is longer than the preceding section.

▶ New growth and good fortune. Bamboo shoots up powerfully and symbolizes wealth.

▶ Spiritual blessing. The bamboo flute represents upliftment and blessing in your life.

The type of flute and the way you hang it are important. The flute should be bamboo, with the ridges of the bamboo sections still intact; avoid using flutes with sanded ridges. The flute is more powerful if its sections get longer and longer over its length — this symbolizes life improving step-by-step.

The flute should be hung from a red ribbon cut to a multiple of 9" in length and have a red tassel hanging from each point where the ribbon is attached. Hang the flute with smaller sections toward the bottom and larger ones toward the top. If your flute cure has some of these characteristics but not all, it will work but not as effectively as it can.

Bamboo flute, showing suggested hanging angle.

⊕ *Create strength and growth in your relationship with a flute.*

Bamboo flutes are a powerful tool you can
use to enhance and strengthen many areas of
your life. When used for Feng Shui cures,
bamboo flutes symbolize and provide many
powerful qualities, including safety and protection, strength, new growth, good fortune, and
spiritual blessing.

These important qualities can be used to
empower your relationship or to help find the
person who's right for you. Perform the flute
cure for your love life by hanging a bamboo
flute in the Marriage Gua of your bedroom.
The correct angle to hang the flute is at 45°,
with the higher end toward the right. The flute
should be hung at eye level or higher. Enhance
the cure by visualizing that your relationship
or marriage is becoming more understanding
and loving, or by seeing a great new partner
arriving.

⊕ *Retain relationship energy by stopping
  "energy leaks."*

If there is an outside door or large window in
the Marriage Gua of your home or bedroom, chi
may be escaping, causing loss of energy in your
relationship. This situation can be adjusted by
hanging a wind chime or faceted crystal ball in
front of the window or doorway. This cure is
also good for creating a brighter, more expansive, and/or more truthful relationship. With
this cure, visualize that your relationship is
becoming empowered, safe, and happy.

✦ *Solidify a flighty relationship with a strong stone or statue.*

If your relationship could use additional depth or grounding, place a solid stone, heavy statue, or other strong object in your bedroom's relationship corner. It will help when doing this cure to visualize your relationship becoming settled and solid.

✦ *Attract a new romance with a red flower.*

To bring a new romantic situation into your life, place a red flower in a white vase in the relationship corner of your bedroom. Upon placing this flower in your room, see in your mind's eye a nicely blooming relationship coming your way.

✦ *Create more peace by choosing Feng Shui colors for your bedroom.*

Your relationship life will be enhanced by choosing the color of your bedroom wisely. The most recommended master bedroom colors are

The Color Peach

Feng Shui teaching recommends that you use the color peach wisely, or avoid it altogether in your bedroom, living room, dining room, and kitchen. Peach initially attracts charisma and romance, but the situation soon turns to discord. If you want to use peach to attract a romance or to help maintain the relationship, change the color to pink soon after the relationship begins. When applying either of these colors to your bedroom, visualize a stable, happy, and long-lasting partnership.

shades of green and blue, which create healing and balance. Avoid dark shades of these colors, which can lead to depression or introversion. A flat or semi-gloss finish on the paint is more calming than a gloss will be. Another useful wall color to help bring love energy into the bedroom is pink. To empower this cure fully, visualize peace, health, and balance.

✷ Bring in new relationship chi by curing your bedroom door.

Energy must flow into your bedroom for a relationship to be attracted to you. Make sure your bedroom door swings easily and is in good repair. It is important to remove all items around the doorway that obstruct the path or hamper the free swinging of the door. For best effects with this cure, visualize new energy and life coming into your relationship. This cure also allows you to speak your truth and to communicate with your partner more freely. Check the Feng Shui door suggestions on pages 63–64 for additional bedroom door tips. (While you're at it, it helps to pay similar attention to all the doors in the house.)

✷ Defuse relationship arguments caused by clashing doors.

Relationship conflicts and arguments can be created if your bedroom door clashes with another door. This can be remedied by placing red tassels on the doorknobs of each door. Visualize as you place the tassels that you are experiencing peace and a harmonious meeting of the voices in your relationship.

⊕ *Create a new relationship by wearing pink clothing.*

By adjusting the colors of your clothes with Feng Shui, you can create changes in your chi and destiny. To create a new relationship, wear pink, the relationship color. (It does not have to be visible.) This cure is stronger if you wear pink clothing for nine days in a row. Visualize that a happy and lasting relationship is coming to you.

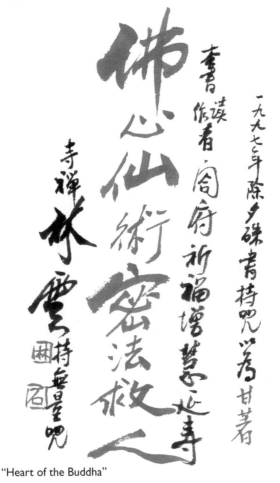

"Heart of the Buddha"

4

Health and Vitality

HEALTH IS CENTRAL IN FENG SHUI, in both importance and placement. Health is an enabler of all parts of your life and is especially connected to wealth. It may be a cliché, but it is true that no matter what our standing, without good health we have very little in life. Professor Lin Yun teaches that your health is associated with the center area of your home, office, and bedroom.

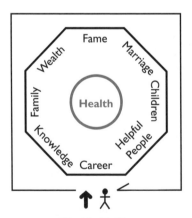

The Health Gua

Method I: Enhance the Vitality Level of Your Environment

⊕ *Create multiple and massive benefits by cleaning.*

One of the most important Feng Shui tips is to clean your home. Yes, good old-fashioned housecleaning is a top method for enhancing the chi of your home and life. Dirt traps an amazing amount of psychic energy in your space, sapping your energy on subtle levels and keeping you unnecessarily stuck. You can enhance the cleanliness level of any Gua of the Ba-Gua that needs a lift.

When you clean, visualize the old energy and problems being swept away, with new, fresh energy and possibilities pouring into your life.

⊕ *Enjoy health and vitality by adding living energy to your bedroom.*

Keeping healthy, living things around you is a key way to enhance your health. The bedroom is a great place for new, lively green plants that will brighten the atmosphere, add the healing color of green, add fresh oxygen, and provide vital energy to your life. This cure has an uplifting effect on your energy, refreshing you physically and enlivening your spirit. Visualize radiant, glowing health and fresh, healthy energy circulating in your body.

⊕ *Improve your health by enhancing the center of your house.*

Strengthening the center strengthens all of life. Earth is the element associated with the Health Gua (see page 77). Bringing the energy of earth into the center strengthens health and all other areas of your life. The energy of the

Plants as Feng Shui Cures

Both living plants and silk plants work well as cures. If you use silk plants, choose those that look the most real. If you use living plants, keep them alive and healthy. If your plants become sick or die, replace them at once with larger and livelier ones. The best plants for cures are those that are lush and rich, with lots of green. (Plants that have sharp, spiky leaves or tines, such as cactus and mother-in-law's tongue, should be avoided.)

earth can be brought to the Health Gua by placing earthen objects (pottery, sculpture, plants in large pots) or by using an earth color: yellow, orange, brown, or tan. For greatest benefit, visualize strengthened health when performing this cure.

⊛ *Awaken new healing energy with a bedroom chime.*

Since the center is the key Gua for health and the bedroom is the room of rest and rejuvenation, enhancing the center of your bedroom is a powerful strategy for boosting your health chi. A wind chime hung from the ceiling in the center of your bedroom will strongly activate your body's physical and emotional health. Use a metal (such as brass) chime with a sound that you enjoy, hung from a red ribbon.

This cure is effective even if there's not enough air moving in the room to ring the chime. Any time you want to give your health or personal energy a boost, make it a point to ring your "health chime," and visualize new forces of health and vitality awakening and circulating throughout your body.

⊕ *Invoke spiritual and physical health with healing or natural images.*

All cultural and spiritual traditions contain certain human or divine personalities whose specialty is healing and the nurturing of the body. These teachers, patron saints, angels, and healing deities have always helped humans who have asked them in time of need. A great way to tap into this timeless energy is to place in your home a painting or sculpture of a healing figure with a special meaning to you. Creating a special place in the home for it to reside, particularly near the center of your home, will increase the healing chi of the environment.

Method II: Protect the Bed and Table for Safety and Health

In addition to the bed placement suggestions given in chapter 3, all of which aid health, the space over your bed is an important health

---

Healing and Natural Images

Each tradition has one or several special personages for healing and health. Select ones that you personally resonate with and reverently invite them into your home as a symbol of your connection and commitment to a higher healing power. A variation of this cure is to use photographs or paintings of nature scenes that look and feel invigorating, nurturing, and deeply healing to you. Photographs of lush green environments, such as forests and jungle scenes, can be particularly helpful.

When you perform this cure, visualize being blessed by a universal healing power, wherever you are.

---

consideration. It is important to balance the effects of oppressively slanted ceilings and beams directly over the bed. If you have either of these situations, your health and fortune will improve by performing these simple cures.

⊕ *Relieve mental stress by adjusting oppressively slanted ceilings.*

Oppressively slanted ceilings are those that slant down to a level lower than a regular ceiling height; generally a ceiling slanting down lower than 6 to 7 feet is considered oppressive. Over the bed, slanted ceilings can cause a depressive effect on personal energy and health. They can also contribute to depression, insomnia, and scattered thinking. A good cure is to hang a faceted crystal ball or small brass bell over the bed, a few inches down from the ceiling. This cure will help disperse the oppressive downward energy and also have the positive benefit of activating your chi. Be sure to hang your crystal ball or bell from a red ribbon that is cut to a multiple of 9" in length. Visualize increased health and freedom from illness as you do this cure.

⊕ *Enhance safety by curing beams directly over the bed.*

Beams over the bed can negatively impact physical and mental health. *A beam running lengthwise* down the bed can cause problems in the midline of the body (if it runs directly over your body); if *a beam is between you and your partner,* it can create division in the relationship. *A beam running across your bed* negatively affects the body parts it crosses over. *A beam over the head of the bed* can create headaches or neck problems; *over the center,* digestive or abdominal issues; *over the feet,* a foot injury.

To cure beams over the bed, hang one crystal

ball or bell from each end of the beam to disperse energy. Also, the color red can be used as a cure, in the form of a red fringe that runs the length of the beam. Add healing energy by running a silk ivy vine the length of the beam.

Beams that run over the dining room table can also have a negative effect on health, career, and the marriage relationship. The cures given here will work to resolve a beam above the dining room table as well as over the bed.

When you perform these cures, visualize that you are free of accidents and disease, and your relationship is protected.

Method III: Use Color Cures for Your Health

⊛ *Boost your bed's vitality with the color red.*

The bed is the place of rest and rejuvenation and offers a multitude of opportunities for Feng Shui health improvement cures. The color red is used in Feng Shui to add healing and curing energy to any situation. An excellent way to boost your energy and vitality is to place a bright red sheet between the mattress and box spring of your bed. As you put this cure in place, visualize the red color boosting your personal energy dramatically, warding off all disease and health problems, and your body glowing with radiant health.

⊛ *Enliven your innate healing chi with green or yellow.*

In addition to wearing the Five Element colors for healing (see page 88), some powerful individual colors can be worn for healing. Wearing green or yellow can assist your health. Green refers to new life and growth, while yellow relates directly to healing energy.

Wearing these colors is especially effective if you visualize them boosting your energy throughout the day. Be sure to use shades that are pleasing to your own tastes. As you wear these colors, visualize increased physical, mental, and emotional health.

⊛ *Create good health with a green or red door.*

Your front door can be painted a nice shade of green as a health and good luck cure for everyone in the household. When the door is painted, visualize that the power of the green color is adding health, vitality, and good fortune to your house and life. (See p. 56 for red door.)

Method IV: Stop Energy Leaks to Retain Household Energy

⊛ *Increase personal energy by keeping bathroom doors closed and mirrored.*

A simple and easy health-boosting cure is to keep your bathroom doors closed. Bathrooms contain several drains that can sap your household and personal energy. The more household chi you conserve, the stronger your own energy will be.

An additional energy-retaining cure is to put full-length mirrors on the outsides of your bathroom doors. This cure is particularly important for a bathroom door that is inside the bedroom or in a hallway leading to the bedroom.

Visualize health and personal energy being increased through the power of this cure.

✤ *Preserve good health by adjusting a bathroom in the center of the house.*

Since health chi is in the center, the center of the house is the most regrettable Feng Shui location for a bathroom. The recommended cure for a central bathroom is to mirror all four inside walls of the bathroom. If you cannot do this, at least mirror the outside of the bathroom door and keep it closed. This is also a good cure for a bathroom located in the Wealth Gua or near the front entrance of the home. Visualize your health improving and your energy being enhanced as you perform these cures.

✤ *Retain energy by keeping drains closed.*

Another good step toward personal energy retention can be taken by keeping all the drains in the house closed when not in use. This is most important for toilets (lids down), but also applies to sinks, tubs, showers, floor drains, washing machines, and other drains in your environment. Most people who do this cure report feeling an immediate and tangible improvement in how they feel. Be sure to visualize increased personal energy in your life when you do this cure.

✤ *Enhance peace and safety by fixing angles and protruding corners.*

Sharp angles and corners that protrude into key rooms, such as bedrooms and living rooms, can have noticeable disturbing effects on your chi and therefore your health. Even a piece of furniture or artwork can jut out and extend "negative chi" into the room. Remedying these situations will enhance the peace and balance of your home. You can cure angles and protruding corners by hanging a crystal ball or a brass bell or by placing a plant in front of the offending angle.

When using this cure, visualize greater health and safety for all in the family.

⊕ *Avoid health problems by healing spiral staircases.*

Spiral staircases are a real health threat, as their corkscrew shape creates a "downward" energy. This feature can be detrimental to physical health and create accidents, injuries, and ill fortune. The negative effect of a spiral staircase is even greater if it has been added since you moved into the house, something to be avoided at all costs. The worst location of all for a spiral staircase is in the center of the house, which is the Health Gua of the home.

Curing the energy of spiral staircases is very important. One or more of the following remedies is suggested:

Wrap a green silk vine around the handrail all the way from the bottom to the top. Green adds the compensating energy of life to the stairway, bringing the influence of vital chi into the space. The feel of the silk vine on your hand as you go up and down will stimulate your sense of touch — a subtle yet effective boost to your immune system.

Empowering Your Cures

The plant and silk vine cures can be integrated and empowered by inserting one end of the silk vine into the potting soil of each plant. The vine now symbolically connects the plants and vine into one system and conducts the chi of the two plants throughout the field of the stairway.

Add a lively green potted plant, the larger the better, both under the stairway and at the top of the stairs. The plant below the stairs will fill up the space and help stop the downward action of the stairs. The plant at the top of the stairs will be a healing sight upon reaching the top and will help "pull" the energy up, assisting your climb. Both plants will create more living and active chi. Even if you can add only one plant rather than two, it is still a helpful cure.

Add a crystal ball above the top of the staircase. It will help harmonize, balance, and uplift the location, nullifying distorting effects that spiral stairs have on human and environmental chi.

While doing these cures, the full effect will be realized if you visualize your chi rising, your health improving, and your body glowing with vitality.

Method V: Use the "Five Elements" for Health and Balance

Health is truly a matter of balance. In Chinese energy theory there are Five Elements that make up all things in the universe, including our bodies: wood, fire, earth, metal, and water. Ancient Chinese medicine states that all human health problems result from an imbalance in the relative amounts of these basic energies in the human body.

Each of the Five Elements represents a unique energetic principle important for balance and health. This way of thinking can be a powerful way to enhance health, peace, and balance. Having all these elements in your environment at once can bring increased harmony and energy into your life.

❀ *Create balance by bringing the Five Elements into a key room.*

The physical representation of an element can be anything that characterizes that element. Use your imagination and creativity. For instance, the fire element can be represented by a fireplace, the wood element by a piece of wooden furniture, the earth element by a piece of pottery or any clay item, the water element by a picture of a river, and the metal element by a metal table.

If the whole family can use health and balance improvement, family-centered rooms such as the living room, family room, and den are good places to perform this cure. If a specific person's health is in need, his or her bedroom is usually the best location for the Five Elements.

This cure can be done by placing a fountain (water), a metal ornament or sculpture (metal), a candle (fire), a clay pot or earthen bowl (earth), and a plant, wooden chair, or table (wood) in the living room, family room, master bedroom, or the bedroom of a person whose health you want to boost.

As you arrange each item, visualize these elements combining and contributing strongly to your health. Also visualize that these elements are helping you balance your body and personal health by correctly adjusting your own internal elements.

❀ *Enliven your health by placing the Five Element colors in a key room.*

Another effective way to enhance your health with powerful energy of the Five Element system is to use a color that represents each of the elements.

These colors can be put into your environment by using a design that contains one color from each element, or you can bring in five items, each one of a different elemental color. This cure is strongly empowered by visualizing that the Five Element colors you have assembled are combining and working together to harmonize and balance your internal organs and physical system, resulting in greatly increased health and balance in your body.

ELEMENT	COLOR CHOICES
Wood	Green, blue, blue-green
Fire	Red
Earth	Yellow, orange, brown, tan
Metal	White
Water	Black, dark blue

⊛ *Fortify your health with Five Elements at the center.*

In the Ba-Gua diagram, the center is the Gua that most affects your health. A particularly powerful variation of the above cure is to gather items or colors from each of the Five Elements and arrange them near the center of your home or bedroom. Those with a strong desire to be very healthy, or with a great need in this area of their life, may do this cure in all three locations: living room, bedroom, and the center of the house.

When you do this cure, visualize balanced, healthy energies radiating from the center to all of your home, family, and life.

⊕ *Spark your vitality by wearing the Five Element colors.*

Wear clothing containing five colors, one from each of the elements. Performing this cure for nine consecutive days will create an increase in balance and healthy chi. Be sure to visualize better health when you are doing this cure.

Method VI: Eliminate Contaminants from Your Home

Modern life choices have inundated our lives and homes with a wealth of conveniences and techno-gadgets that carry with them unexamined materials. Use these tips to protect yourself against modern household health invasions. As you perform any of these beneficial cures, visualize that the power of the cure is enhancing and protecting your health.

⊕ *Reduce stress by keeping electrical items away from the bed.*

The Feng Shui condition around where you sleep is vital for physical health and well-being. Electrical devices are of particular importance. Alarm clocks, radios, tape players, clock radios, and dimmer switches located near the bed can secretly affect your health. They emit powerful electromagnetic fields that zap vitality and lower resistance to disease.

Enhance your health by moving your electrical appliances 24" to 36" or more away from your body. Another option is to replace them with battery-powered substitutes. Waterbed heaters and electric blankets are especially negative to health. Minimize their effects by turning them on 30 to 60 minutes before going to bed and then unplugging them before you go to bed.

❋ *Reduce stress by cleansing your home of EMFs.*

Electromagnetic fields (EMFs) have a disturbing influence on human energy fields, creating confusion, physical energy loss, and possibly a weakened immune system. Our homes are bathed in these invisible fields from a multitude of known and unknown sources.

To know for certain the EMF levels around your house, check the fields with a hand-held gaussmeter, which measures the intensity of

Basic EMF Protection Checklist

▸ Move all appliances 36" or more away from the bed, including clock radios. Battery-operated models are a good substitute.

▸ Unplug electric blankets and waterbed heaters before getting into bed.

▸ Install a demand switch that can turn off all electrical power to the bedroom at night.

▸ Remove neon and fluorescent lights from your space. Replace fluorescents with full spectrum tubes or incandescent lights.

▸ Make sure your electrical system is correctly wired and grounded (typically to the water system) according to code.

▸ Use a computer display (CRT) that is compliant with TCO 95, the world's strictest specification for ergonomic protection from computer radiation. A glare and radiation screen is also very helpful when added to your computer display. Keep your computer system (which contains the CPU) off your desktop and at least 30" away from your body. If you are highly sensitive, get a CPU and keyboard that are also TCO 95–compliant.

EMFs. The recommended field level is 1 mG (milligauss) or lower.

✺ *Filter your air for better health.*

Air quality is a top health issue. The mass media have publicized the fact that the air inside your home may be two to ten times more polluted than outdoor city air. Air filters are the weapon of choice in this battle. A good HEPA-certified air filter costs $300–$800 and removes loads of unhealthy smoke, fumes, particulates, and dust. HEPA is a filtering standard designed to catch allergens and many other irritants.

✺ *Improve your life dramatically by cleaning your water.*

Your body can absorb as much water in a 10-minute shower as if you drank 16 ounces. Because water is one of the most important things we take in, water quality is an important health issue. The quality of tap water in many cities in the United States is questionable; you can usually get yours tested by an independent lab for a nominal fee. The recommended cure is to filter your water, although a little research may be in order. A full-house water filtration system is the ideal solution, but can run $800–$5,000 to install. Instead, a high-quality shower filter that removes chlorine and lead from the water is a good starting point. Drinking-water filters are a basic need in almost every home. Reverse osmosis filtration is one of the best drinking-water solutions, but is more expensive than an activated carbon filter, which removes sediment, chlorine, and some of the major poisons. A newcomer to the water-filtering scene is the *microwater filter,* which changes the pH of the water to a level highly beneficial for your health.

⬤ *Enjoy a cleaner feeling home with a HEPA vacuum cleaner.*

Your regular vacuum cleaner pulls this stunt: It sucks dirt from the carpet and retains the larger pieces, but then simply pulverizes the rest of the dirt and parasites and spews the mixture (invisibly) back into the air, where it can be inhaled. Change this state of affairs by switching to hardwood floors or, less expensive, get a high-quality HEPA-certified vacuum cleaner, which actually cleans the air in addition to the floors. Your lungs will thank you.

⬤ *Improve your immune system by removing toxic chemicals from your house.*

Modern cleaning chemicals also bring a host of subtly damaging fumes into the home. You are probably keeping many of these items under the kitchen sink, which can also add a subtle negative essence to the cooking process.

To reduce the physical stress created by this, replace standard brands of dish soap and laundry soap with natural-based alternatives. Get rid of toxic cleansers by replacing them with natural brands that are much safer for you, better for your health, and friendlier to the environment.

⬤ *Increase personal energy by removing the parasites from your carpet.*

Awareness has been greatly heightened in recent years regarding household parasites and dust mites. Their favorite hideout is your carpet, but they also hold major outposts in your couch, bed, and pillows. Fight back and feel much better physically and psychologically with a HEPA vacuum cleaner. You can mount an even more effective assault with several products now available for killing and removing parasites from the home. They typically feature a natural-based substance that is brushed into the carpet and vacuumed up after a few hours, bringing parasites with it for disposal.

Method VII: Control Your Weight

⊕ *Balance eating patterns with a crystal over the dining room table.*

Crystals are a key tool for creating clarity and balance. A faceted crystal ball hung over the dining room table (hang with red ribbon, 9" or a multiple in length) can bring balance to your eating patterns. This cure also aids family harmony.

For best effects when doing this cure, mentally picture yourself looking great, feeling healthy, and quickly attaining the weight you desire, with greater willpower aiding you.

⊕ *Control eating patterns with a mirror on the refrigerator door.*

Weight control can be assisted by the addition of a mirror on the refrigerator door. This cure works on two levels: On the conscious level, a mirror on the door makes you see yourself each time you head for food. A look at your image may reduce your intake level. Energetically, the mirror can "push you away" from excess eating, giving you more control and balance with food intake.

When putting this mirror in place, visualize ease and control over your eating habits.

⊕ *Promote weight loss by wearing the
color white.*

Professor Lin Yun suggests wearing white to
lose weight. The secret to this cure could lie in
reverse psychology: Since white makes you look
larger, you may be compelled to curb eating.
Visualize that you are quickly attaining your
ideal weight and shape.

"Yin and Yang"

5

Business and Career

IN THIS CHAPTER, many powerful tips are given for using Feng Shui to enhance your business and career. These business and career tips will help whether you are the owner of a large or small business, work for a company, or work out of your home. Even if you work at home, positioning and placement in your home office definitely affect your career opportunities and your success.

The chi of your business needs to be awake, lively, and uplifting to create success. The entrance must be attractive and beckoning if you want to bring in deals, clients, and sales. Work to transform "dead" and stagnant chi into living and bright chi as soon as possible.

Placement of key individuals in the company is another important area to pay close attention to. For your personal career, doing cures in your individual office and in the Career Guas of your home and bedroom will improve your odds of success.

The Ba-Gua for Business

Although the principles of the Ba-Gua and its placement are the same for your business building as for your home (see page 27), when applying the Ba-Gua to your business, additional "life areas" are added to some of the Guas.

Gua	Home Areas	Additional Areas for Business
Front right corner	Helpful people	Employees, customers, suppliers
Front center	Career	Same
Front left corner	Knowledge, growth	Information, data
Middle left side	Family	Employees, customers
Back left corner	Wealth	Same
Back center	Fame	Vision, reputation, marketing
Back right corner	Marriage	Business partnership
Middle right side	Children, creativity	Employees, communication
Center	Health	Same

Applying the Ba-Gua to Your Business's Floor Plan

By placing the Ba-Gua diagram on your business's floor plan, you can identify which parts of the building to rush to and immediately begin doing important Feng Shui cures. (If your company rents part of a building [an office suite], the Ba-Gua applies only to the portion you lease, not the entire building.) Overlay the Ba-Gua on your business floor plan the same as

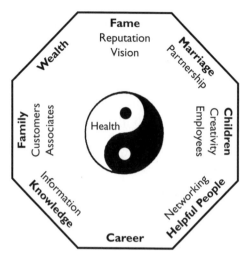

Ba-Gua for business with additional life areas

with your home floor plan: according to the location of the Mouth of Chi (main front door of the building). Always place the Helpful People, Career, and Knowledge Guas of the Ba-Gua right, center, and left, respectively, along the front wall of the building, which is the wall containing the Mouth of Chi. (Please see page 26 for more on how to position the Ba-Gua.)

Applying the Ba-Gua to Your Personal Office

The Ba-Gua also applies to your individual office, whether it be a home office or located at a job site. According to the Theory of Relative Positioning, the Ba-Gua of your personal office has even more effect on your life and destiny than the Ba-Gua of the entire building. Virtually all the cures given in this chapter can be effectively applied to the Ba-Gua of your individual office (along with using them for the Ba-Gua of the building).

Method I: Enhance the Energy of Your Business

Here are nine "quick-and-easy" cures you can implement to change the energy and results of your business. The Guas used can be from the Ba-Gua of either your building or your individual office. For maximum effectiveness, be sure to visualize in detail your desired success while performing these cures.

⊕ *Promote harmony in the company family with plants.*

Place healthy green plants in the entrance or Family Gua of the business to promote peace and unity among all members of the organization. This cure is also good for sales.

⊕ *Stimulate and magnify wealth with a chime or mirror.*

In the Wealth Gua of your building or office, place a wind chime to stimulate money energy, or a mirror to draw it in and expand it.

⊕ *Strengthen the health of your business and that of your employees.*

In the center of the building, place fresh green plants or hang a crystal ball with a red ribbon. This cure strengthens all parts of the business simultaneously and helps boost health.

⊕ *Attract more helpers with sound or mobile energy.*

Hang a wind chime or mobile in your Helpful People Gua or near the entrance to stimulate more people helping you — more of the time — in your business.

⊕ *Enhance creativity, communication, and organization with a crystal ball.*

Hang a faceted crystal ball from a red ribbon (9" long or a multiple) in the Children Gua to improve creativity. Another cure is to put something metal, something white, or a mobile in the Children Gua to stay organized and keep communication flowing.

⊕ *Stimulate knowledge and intelligence with light.*

Place a bright light or a mobile in the Knowledge Gua of the business to stimulate better thinking and information gathering.

⊕ *Brighten the company reputation with red.*

To spread the word about your company far and wide, place something bright and red in the Fame Gua, such as red flowers or artwork.

⊕ *Enhance career and cash flow with flowing water.*

Place an aquarium or fountain (or both) in the front entryway or Career Gua of your building.

⊕ *Strengthen an internal or external business partnership with a flute.*

Hang a bamboo flute in the Marriage Gua to strengthen, clarify, and harmonize your primary business partnership. (See page 72 on hanging your flute.)

Method II: Enhance the Key Location — The Boss's Office

The location, arrangement, and overall Feng Shui of the head person's office (owner, president, or manager) is an extremely important aspect of your business success. The decisions, actions, and attitudes of the boss affect everyone connected with the company, both inside and outside the firm. If the Feng Shui of the boss's office is powerful, the boss is likely to act with wisdom, authority, and balance. As a result, the company has the opportunity to prosper. If the Feng Shui of the boss's office is weak, the boss will be weakened and company fortunes can suffer.

Here are cures to ensure the luck and success of the head of your company. If you are not in a head position, you can still use these "head person" cures to advance your own career.

⊕ *Empower the boss in the building's Commanding Position.*

The job of the boss is to run the company. More responsibility for the company's success is on his or her shoulders than on anyone else's. It is fitting, then, that the boss's office be located in the most powerful part of the building. This position is called the Commanding Position by Professor Lin Yun. Your company's fortunes will be powerfully enhanced by moving the head person to a Commanding Position area.

If practical considerations make it impossible to put the boss's office in an ideal Feng Shui position, a substitute cure is to place a picture of the boss where the office would ideally be located, or use a mirror to pull the boss's energy farther into the building. If an office manager needs more authority, he or she can be moved into the Commanding Position or at least into a more powerful position using principles in the box on page 101.

As with all your cures, for maximum results visualize that proper decisions are being made and the company is successful.

The Commanding Position

The best position is the office farthest from the front door. If the boss sits near the front of the building, he or she can easily be weakened and inundated. In addition, the office should ideally be:

▶ Located in either the Wealth or Partnership (Marriage) Gua.

▶ In the safest and most protected location in the building.

▶ The largest and most prestigious office in the company.

▶ Located away from a bathroom or a back door.

Method III: Enhance Your Business's Entrance and Wealth Gua

The entrance of a business is a vital location to cure with Feng Shui, since it is the point where energy must come in for the company to thrive. The Wealth Gua, located in the far left section of the building, is also a very important Feng Shui location for the success of any business.

Cures given in this book for the Mouth of Chi (main front entrance) and for the Wealth Guas of the home will work for your business as well (see pages 113–119, 46–48, respectively).

✦ *Magnify your business prosperity with wind chimes, plants, and moving water.*

Both the entrance and the Wealth Guas can benefit from the addition of chimes (to stimulate and activate chi, money, and people), plants (to create lively, attractive, and healing chi), and moving water, such as fountains, streams, or waterfalls (to stimulate the production and circulation of cash). These cures will be maximized if you visualize in great detail the success of your business plans.

⊕ *Brighten spirits by placing flowers in three key places.*

A great cure to raise the spirits of the troops and enhance the luck of the company is to put fresh flowers in the manager's office, reception area, and employee lounge. Be sure to exchange the flowers for new ones as soon as they begin to lose their freshness. When doing this cure, it is suggested to strongly visualize fresh energy, success, and prosperity arriving now.

Method IV: Place Your Desk in the Best Position

Desk positioning is a key Feng Shui matter for your career success. The ideal desk position will conform to the Commanding Position principle, similar to that described in chapter 3 for optimal bed placement. (See illustration on page 64.)

⊕ *Control your career and life by sitting in the Commanding Position.*

In the Commanding Position, your desk can sit at an angle or with your back to either wall. The choice of corner to place your desk in depends on whether your entrance is in the Helpful People, Career, or Knowledge Gua of your office. This means that you will be in either the Wealth or Partnership area of your office. These are the most powerful parts of your office and create fortune and blessing for your career and wealth. Visualize great success as you move your desk position using the following four principles.

⊕ *Strengthen your position by sitting as far from the door as possible.*

The more room between you and the door, the better. This keeps you from feeling inundated or overwhelmed by tasks and people. This position gives you "more territory," expands safety, and increases your reaction time to deal with opportunities and problems as they arise.

⊕ *Increase your awareness by facing the door.*

It is important to face your office door with the majority of the room in view. This guideline lets you know who's coming when and keeps you up to date with what's going on in your company. It increases your ability to concentrate and keeps you from being startled by events that occur during the workday. If you can't face the door, a substitute cure is to place a mirror so that you can see the door just by glancing up from your work.

Desk Positioning

Upon hearing these principles of desk placement, some people think that they don't have feelings of insecurity; they are always aware of what's happening even though their backs have been toward the door for years. Others feel that by keeping their backs to the door, they are interrupted less often and are able to get more work done in less time. This is a common and unfortunate Feng Shui error that results from not even being aware of insecurities and interruptions that are subconsciously sapping one's energy and keeping one from being fully effective. Upon turning their desks toward the door, clients feel greatly empowered, freer, and more in command of their careers.

⊕ *Feel stronger by keeping your back
to a solid wall.*

This protects you and increases your feeling
of security, strengths, and poise. Don't back your
desk so close to the wall that you don't have
room to get out from behind your desk freely.

⊕ *Don't "box yourself in" against a wall.*

Don't place your desk so close to one wall that
you can get to it only from one side. A freestanding desk is more powerful and independent than
one that's up against a wall. Being able to access
your desk from both sides helps you have more
flexibility and creativity in your career — resulting in more autonomy and control.

Method V: Cure Your Desk and Office Chair for Success

⊕ *Check the size, condition, and "predecessor"
of your desk.*

If you inherit a desk, pay close attention to
who sat there before you came along, and why
he or she left. If the previous occupant was dis-
liked, attacked, demoted, fired, or left because
of sickness, death, legal issues, family troubles,
or any other negative reason, your desk can still
retain his or her "unlucky chi." This chi may
affect you and create similar troubles for you.

The best cure for an unlucky desk is to
replace it with a new one as soon as possible. If
this is not possible, the recommended cure is to
place a new and lively green plant near where
you sit to compensate for unlucky chi. As you
first sit down at your new desk or put your
plant into place, visualize success and happiness in your new job.

New vs. Old

Getting a new desk rather than sitting at a used one is better for your career in almost every circumstance. One exception is inheriting a desk from a predecessor who was successful, wealthy, or promoted, for this can give you a career boost. Another exception is replacing a desk with a new one that is oddly shaped, uncomfortable, too small, badly placed, or lacking a full front panel. These shortcomings mean you are exchanging one set of problems for another. New is better.

❀ *Protect yourself with a full front desk panel.*

An important desk principle is to be sure that the front panel of your desk extends all the way to the floor. This provides solid protection, a better reputation, and a "good front" behind which you can produce superior work. Less than a full panel creates career vulnerabilities, especially in the way others see you. When doing this cure, visualize that you are protected on all levels and that your reputation is always improving.

❀ *Expand your vision with a larger desk.*

Expand your vision, ideas, and career powerfully by sitting at a desk that is spacious, symbolically expanding the room for your ideas and projects. However, a sense of proportion is recommended for this cure. Your desk should not be so huge that it engulfs the room, leaving little room to walk around in your office. With this cure, visualize the growth of your career and see your fortunes expanding.

⊕ *Boost your career with a crystal over your sitting position.*

To create overall benefit for your career, or to protect yourself from attack, hang a crystal ball (from a red ribbon 9" in length or a multiple) over your head where you sit at your desk. This important and powerful basic cure can aid you in many ways: clearer thinking, better decisions, and a brighter outlook on your future. Another way to perform this cure is to hang the crystal over the center of your desk. The brightness of the crystal ball and its multiple facets create expansion of your career and projects. If you are adventurous, you can hang crystals in both locations. Visualize that you are experiencing the above benefits when you put your crystal(s) in place.

⊕ *Enhance interpersonal harmony with a crystal ball on your desk.*

Placing a crystal ball on your desk can promote harmony between you and your coworkers, especially if tension exists or if you are under a lot of pressure at your workplace. Where to place the crystal ball on your desk? Between you and the door of your office, between you and oncoming traffic, or between

---

Two Cures to Perform for Employee Harmony

1. Place three green plants in the main entry and in the entry where the employees come in.
2. Place a large octagonal mirror in the Children or Helpful People Guas of your company building.

As you place these cures, visualize harmonious activity among everyone.

---

you and the desk of a person you need to get along better with. When you do this cure, visualize yourself having harmonious relationships with everyone in the company.

⊕ *Stimulate creativity at your desk with a brass bell.*

An easy way to stimulate your creative powers and give your communication skills a boost is to place a brass bell in the center right section of your desk (Children Gua). Ring it when you need a creative boost and visualize receiving the solution you need.

⊕ *Sit in the catbird seat with a "fortunate" chair.*

The chair you sit in when working is another important element of your career success, one that is even closer to you than your desk.

As always in Feng Shui, "fresh is best," so a brand-new chair is preferred. An alternative to this principle is to inherit a chair from a successful predecessor. If you like your job and want to keep it, don't use a chair previously used by a failed or fired predecessor. If your company won't purchase you a new one, it's worth it to spend your own money and get yourself a brand-new chair.

Sitting in a solid-backed chair, with no gap between the back part and the seat part of the chair, means you will have support, strong backing, and protection in your work. A chair with an opening in the back leaves you unsupported and open for secret "energy arrows" from people envious of your success. Small or rickety chairs should be avoided; the energy can make the occupant "stay small" in his or her career. It's no accident that solid, tall, and powerful chairs are called "executive" chairs, while smaller and more vulnerable chairs are called "secretary" chairs.

When doing any of these key Feng Shui chair cures, for best results visualize your success, advancement, and prosperity increasing.

Chair Backs

The height of your chair back also relates to your success. It is recommended that the back of your chair go up at least to shoulder level for strength and protection. If the back extends as high as the top of your head, this is even stronger.

Method VI: Adjust the Career Guas of Your Home

The Career Gua of your home or bedroom is the front center section of the Ba-Gua on your floor plan. Cures you perform in this Gua will help boost your career and business success.

⊕ *Expand your career with flowing water.*

Water is the element associated with the Career Gua, so placing moving water in this part of your home is a recommended cure. Moving water increases your contacts and social interaction, helps your career move, and brings flowing money into your life. Place a fountain in the Career Gua of your home, especially near the front door (without blocking it), and watch things begin to move more quickly for you.

As you put your fountain in place, visualize in detail your career growing and expanding, with many people helping you.

⊕ *Awaken career energy with a wind chime.*

If movement, activation, and awakening are desired in your career, a wind chime in this location will set lots of new energy in motion,

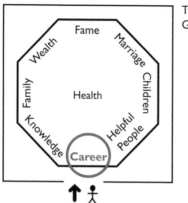

The Career Gua

activate your personal chi, and call forth your message. Be sure to choose a chime made of metal, with a strong, clear, and pleasant sound. This chime can be placed in the Career Gua of your home or of your bedroom, or in both areas. Chimes should be hung with a red ribbon, cut to a multiple of 9" in length.

Visualize many new and positive things happening in your career as you perform this cure.

Create a growing career with living chi generators.

One of the best ways to add new life to your career is with healthy, new plants, but realistic-looking silk plants work as well. Placing an odd number of plants in the career section of your home or your bedroom will create nourishing, growing energy in this area of your life.

Another option for adding living energy is with bird feeders, which can be placed outside next to the career area of your home. With this cure, it is beneficial to visualize the growth and career results you want, as you set your plants or feeders into place.

Method VII: Additional Business and Career Cures

⊕ *Expand your thinking with a set of mirrors.*

A pair of well-placed mirrors will help expand your lateral thinking and creativity. Here are three good places to install a pair of mind-expanding mirrors:

▸ On the walls on either side of your desk.
▸ On both sides of your entry at home (inside), so you pass between them as you enter your home. This is especially good if your entry-way is narrow.
▸ On both sides of the main entrance of the company building or your personal office.

As you install these mirrors, their effect will be heightened if you visualize that your thinking is being expanded and stimulated. Each time you pass between them, again visualize that you are constantly opening new avenues of creativity and lateral thinking. Excellent, prosperity-bringing ideas are pouring into your head now.

⊕ *Enhance your image with a red flower.*

A quick, easy way to enhance the good name and image of your company is to place flowers in the center of the wall opposite your desk. Visualize the word spreading and customers calling.

⊕ *Enhance focus and concentration with a chime.*

To awaken additional focus, concentration, and creative powers, hang a wind chime over the center of your desk. Visualize high productivity and correct action taken.

✪ Increase creativity with a mobile.

To enhance the flow of new ideas, place a gently moving mobile over your head at the location where you sit at your desk. Visualize creative solutions streaming into your brain on a continuous basis.

✪ Eliminate troubles in computer and telephone systems.

Hang a large faceted crystal ball in the center of the computer room or above a problem workstation. A troublesome section of your network will benefit from a wind chime hanging over it to disperse negative chi. Visualize a smooth and prosperous flow of data and communication.

✪ Spread the word about you with sound.

To help more people hear about your company and its products or services, hang a wind chime in the center of your conference room. Visualize a tidal wave of positive publicity about your company hitting your market.

✪ Keep the troops moving by putting the soldiers in the front.

To keep your salespeople working and active, place them in offices or desks near the front door, rather than in the back of the building. Visualize that they are connected to what's happening with their customers and prospects.

✪ Enhance company fortunes and decision making by placing the director's chair auspiciously.

Place the company director's or chairman's chair in the most powerful position in the conference room, which is the farthest from the door and at the head of the table. Visualize all the success you desire.

⊕ *Bring in more money by strengthening the cash register.*

For retail businesses, enhancing the cash register helps increase and protect your wealth. A mirror beside or behind the cash register symbolizes doubled sales. A plant nearby brings lively energy to your cash flow. When using these cures, visualize greater income.

"Feng Shui in Harmony with Nature is the Best Feng Shui."

—————— 6 ——————

Opportunities

AN OPPORTUNITY CAN BE DEFINED as a new and welcome possibility for your life. The Feng Shui of your home and office plays a major role in determining which opportunities reach you. Sometimes the opportunities we deserve are "blocked" from reaching us because of the unfortunate Feng Shui of our environments.

This chapter focuses on the importance of the Mouth of Chi, or main front entrance. This part of your house is important not only for the opportunities in your life, but also for wealth, health, and general well-being.

Method I: Expand and Clear the Pathways That Lead to You

The front door of your house, known in Feng Shui as the Mouth of Chi, is the symbolic point for new opportunities to come into your life. All aspects of your entryway, including the front door, doorway, and the path leading to the door, are important locations to cure in order to maximize your Feng Shui for opportunities.

Each residence has only one Mouth of Chi, and this refers to the main front entrance even if you use another door more often. This location is the point where energy enters your home.

It is difficult to overstate the great importance of the Mouth of Chi in your life. The door is a powerful life metaphor, defining the boundary between the inside and outside realms of existence. The ideal Feng Shui for your front door and entry is bright, luminous, clear, and well balanced. The basic principles of good front door Feng Shui are:

▸ The path to the door is clear.
▸ The condition and appearance of the door are good.
▸ Everything works smoothly and well.

The following front entry cures will help you bring into your life all the good opportunities, people, and things you deserve.

✸ *Increase opportunities by ensuring that your address and door are easy to find.*

Make sure the numbers of your address can be read clearly from the street. This helps money and opportunities know where to find you. If your house is too far back from the road for a visible address, make sure the address is on the mailbox clearly, or create a small sign at your driveway entrance stating your family name and address. Some opportunity seekers go so far as to put lighted address number signs on the house or at the drive. When you do these cures, visualize that your presence is known and opportunities come to you easily.

✸ *Open up your life by freeing your door.*

If the door sticks, scrapes or pulls on the floor or rug, hidden obstacles and sticking points will exist in your life. The cure is to shave a fraction of an inch off the bottom of

> ### **"Hidden Front Doors"**
>
> If your door cannot easily be seen from the street, opportunities and income have a harder time getting to you. This situation is called "Hidden Front Door" and can negatively affect your wealth, helpful people, health, and other life areas. (The problem can be even worse if the house faces away from the street.) The cure is to "lead the chi" to your front door by placing lights or mobile objects (flags, wind socks) along the path to the door to bring the energy up to the front entrance. Visualize, upon making these changes, that you are easily found and receive many positive opportunities.

the door to allow it to swing freely. Visualize opening up to life.

⊕ *Increase flow with widely opening door.*

Doors that open less than 90° symbolize being less than 100 percent open to wealth, energy, and opportunity coming to you. This door situation creates subtle hindrances in your life that impede the flow of good things. The cure is to do whatever is necessary to get your door to open 90° or more. Visualize flowing opportunities and income.

⊕ *Prevent hidden obstacles and arguments by clearing the area around doors.*

It is also important that the spaces just outside and inside your front door are free of obstruction. Coats, books, shoes, bicycles, for example, should be cleared out from behind and around the door. These kinds of obstructions create stumbling blocks, frustrations, and hidden obstacles to meeting your goals. Outside the front door, be sure that any newspapers, boxes, plants, and other objects blocking your way are removed so your door and path are clear. The feeling of energy and clarity will be refreshing and invigorating on many levels. Visualize that blocks and hindrances have been removed from your life.

⊕ *Hear opportunity calling with working doorbells.*

If you have a doorbell, it should work and be heard clearly throughout the house. If it is not working, it symbolizes missed opportunity and being closed to the world. If the doorbell has an irritating or broken sound, it stimulates unconscious frustrations. It is recommended to repair these situations immediately for your benefit. You may even want to replace the doorbell with a melodious chime that you enjoy. Visualize that each time it sounds, you are being awarded new gifts and business opportunities.

When performing any of the door cures, best results come when you clearly visualize that opportunities are now coming to you easily and profitably.

Door Tips

In addition to helping you with opportunities, all door tips are important for the rest of your life as well. Not adhering to good Feng Shui door principles can create blocks in your life areas of income, health, self-image, and your ability to speak freely. The opportunity potential of your household will definitely be enhanced by improving all of your door conditions.

Method II: Add Generators to Attract More Incoming Opportunity

When the pathways and doors into your home are open, free, and in good condition, energy and prosperity can flow in freely, enhancing your life in many ways. With the way clear, now you can bring in even more energy by adding "energy generators" near the Mouth of Chi, which will boost the level of chi flowing to you. These helpful cures attract and direct positive chi into your life, resulting in increased opportunities. Outside the front door and between the street and the front door are key points for placing energy generators to build opportunity chi.

Door Condition Checklist

DOOR CONDITION	RESULT
Scrapes on floor	Frustration, blocked energy
Hard to open	Frustration, blocked energy, career problems
Hard to close	Difficult to get paid, complete tasks
Hinges squeak	Problems, fears, and worries
Doesn't fit properly in frame	Life is imbalanced and "off"
Broken window or screen	Decaying life energy
Loose or wobbly	Instability in life
Knob is loose	Hard to get a handle on life
Swings open or shuts by itself	Unstable life
Paint chipping or peeling	Decaying, depressing chi

Additional important door cures are given in chapter 7, pages 126–128.

✷ *Bring opportunity your way by hanging a wind chime outside your front door.*

Opportunities and good fortune will be enhanced by putting an energy "activator" outside your front door. Placing a wind chime outside the front door of your home (or office) is a powerful, basic life cure that can increase opportunities, enhance your luck, protect your home, build your career, and add good cheer to your life. Strongly visualize the above benefits occurring as you hang your chime.

Wind Chimes

It is recommended that you use metal wind chimes (brass is a favorite) rather than wood, ceramic, glass, or tile chimes. It is key that the sound of the chime be pleasant and one that you like. The chime should be in good condition, not rusty or broken. The chime need not ring often for it to be an effective cure. Professor Lin Yun strongly suggests that wind chimes be hung from a red ribbon or cord that is cut to a length of 9" or a multiple of 9. Wind chimes can also be a powerful cure when used inside the house.

✷ *Bring in more opportunity with a new path.*

It is considered more fortunate if the walkway leading to your front door extends to the street. This is better than a walkway that connects only to the driveway. If your walk doesn't go to the street, building another path enhances your opportunities. If you already have a connected walkway, you can create a second pathway, which symbolically brings more chi to the front door, boding well for life in general. When you have built your new path, visualize benefits and income coming to you from many sources.

✦ *Bring in more customers by seeding the path to your door.*

A nicely symbolic cure to attract clients to your business and helpful people to your home is to sprinkle birdseed along the path from your front door to the street. The key to this cure is to visualize that the birdseed is attracting clients and helpful people to you in increasing numbers.

Method III: Seal Your Environment against "Energy Leaks"

After clearing your energy blocks and generating more incoming opportunities, it is important to make your environment free of energy-draining leaks. The following are some main energy leaks.

Bathroom by the front door. This can lead to incoming energy being lost before it has a chance to feed the house and you. The cure is to place a full-length mirror on the front of the bathroom door and to keep the door closed. Visualize retaining your money and energy.

Bathroom in wealth corner. Wealth can go down the drain. Use same cure as above.

Bathroom in center of house. This can cause a draining effect on your whole life, and is very important to cure. Recommended solution: Mirror all four inner walls of the bathroom. Visualize health and all of life being strengthened.

Front door leads straight to back door or large window. Energy can run straight through the house and out the back, without nourishing the home. Place a crystal or wind chime halfway between the front and back doors to spread the beneficial chi around the house. Visualize energy, money, and opportuntiies being retained by your household.

⊕ *Retain income by fixing a stairway in front of the Mouth of Chi.*

If your home has a stairway directly facing the front door, your wealth situation can suffer. The metaphor at work here is that the wealth energy can enter your home, then roll right back out, leaving you less than rich. Ideally, the distance between the door and the beginning of the stairs will be at least twice the height of the master of the home. If the distance is shorter, the recommended cure is to hang a brass wind chime or a faceted crystal ball halfway between the front door and the stairway. Use a red ribbon cut to a multiple of 9" in length. Visualize with this cure that wealth is growing and being retained in your life.

⊕ *Harvest opportunities by sealing the power corners.*

If leaks exist in your Marriage or Wealth Guas, hard-won opportunities could slip away just before fruition. A chime or crystal in front of an exit or window in these locations can retain this important energy for you. When you place this cure, be sure to visualize the prosperous completion of your dreams and projects.

"Feng Shui"

7

Family and Children

ACCORDING TO FENG SHUI, all the Guas of your home's Ba-Gua (see page 29) have their effect on the family area of your life. In fact, one of the best ways to improve your family's harmony and stability is to do as much Feng Shui as possible. Three specific Guas strongly connected to your family's destiny are Family, Children, and Marriage. Since Marriage cures are given in chapter 3, this chapter will focus on the life areas and Guas of Family and Children.

The influence of the Family Gua (middle of the left side of house, bedroom, or yard) concerns mainly your immediate family. Other important aspects of this Gua are extended family, elders, ancestors, and community.

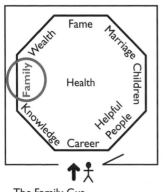

The Family Gua

The Children Gua

The Children Gua is connected with creative energy of all kinds. It relates mainly to your physical children, but also impacts creative projects and communication.

Method I: Enhance the Family Gua of the House

❀ *Calm chaotic energy by placing a gently moving mobile.*

If family energy is unsettled or chaotic, you can calm and balance the situation by placing a gently moving mobile in the Family Gua of the house. As you hang your mobile with a red ribbon (a multiple of 9" long), visualize the gently flowing chi of the mobile calming the household and guiding the family in a peaceful life pattern.

❀ *Enliven and strengthen your family with sound energy.*

The chi of everyone can be enlivened and activated by hanging a wind chime in the Family Gua of the house. Use a red ribbon that is a multiple of 9" long for this chime; the chime should be metal and have a pleasant, clear sound. Visualize your family being stronger and more united as you place the chime.

❀ *Create family health and peace by using "green" energy.*

Qualities that characterize healthy families are harmony, peace, and growth. These qualities will be boosted if you put something with the color green in the Family Gua of the house or the master bedroom. A good choice is healthy, new green plants, but anything with the color

green will help. With this cure, visualize everyone growing together in a very strong and
healthy manner.

Method II: Empower Children's Chi

When using Feng Shui to empower and assist
your children, the prime places to do cures are
the Children Gua of each child's bedroom and
the Children Gua of the house. To strengthen
parenting skills and your connection to your
children, cures can be done in the Children Gua
of your bedroom.

✸ *Improve children overall by placing their beds "fortunately."*

One of the most recommended cures to
strengthen a child's energy is to place the bed in
the Children Gua of the room. This cure places
them in the prime location for their development and maturation. However, make sure that
the bed is not in a direct line with the doorway,
or your child can feel under attack and unsafe.

Be sure to visualize your child becoming
stronger when you put the bed into position.

✸ *Brighten your child's life with a well-placed light.*

Another great way to enhance the growth of
your child is to place a bright light in the
Children Gua of his or her bedroom. This cure
will also help your child communicate better
and be more creative. The light need not be on
continually, but it should be in good working
condition. This cure is especially valuable if the
bed cannot be placed in the Children Gua (see
above). Visualize your child growing and developing brightly as you perform this cure.

⊕ Awaken a child's chi with sound.

The power of sound is another tool that works well for children. A bell or wind chime can awaken their energy, enhancing creativity, protecting them, and bringing harmony into their lives. Use a metal chime with a sound pleasant to the child. Other options you may use are a telephone, radio or tape player, or a stereo speaker. This cure also helps stimulate your child's brain for brighter thinking, increased intelligence, studying more, and doing better on tests.

A great place to hang the wind chime (with a red ribbon) or place other sound cures is in the Knowledge Gua of the child's bedroom or, for even more direct activation of energy, over the head of the bed (if practical). Visualize your child being alert, awake, and strengthened in every way when you place this sound generator.

⊕ Improve the health of a child with plants.

To help your child be healthier or recover from an illness, green plants are highly recommended. Place an odd number (3, 5, and 9 are good) of healthy, newly purchased green plants in the bedroom, with the intention that the child will be healed and strong. For an even stronger cure, you can also put some plants in the Children Gua of the house, master bedroom, and yard. This variation is enhanced if the plants you put in your Children Guas have white flowers, for white is the color of the Children Gua.

For maximum results, visualize your child possessing boundless health and springing vitality.

⊕ Maintain connection with children with a brass bell.

To stay connected to a child absent from home, hang a brass bell from a red ribbon in the Children Gua of your house or master bedroom.

When you do this cure, visualize that you can communicate with and see your child as much as you need to.

Method III: Improve "Family" Rooms

You can improve the chi and happiness of your family by paying attention to the rooms where the family spends time together, such as the living room, dining room, den, and family room. Any effort to make these rooms more pleasant and comfortable will help family harmony.

✦ *Encourage family happiness with color, light, and beauty.*

You can enhance the chi of your family by brightening and beautifying rooms where the family gathers. Wall colors can be altered to create peace and healing. Green and blue are excellent colors for family rooms. Additional color cures to improve the chi include using the Five, Six, or Seven Color System in one of these rooms. (See page 87 for specific ways of using these color systems.)

Adding lights or crystal balls to these rooms can help brighten spirits and improve the health of your household's members. Visualize family harmony, health, and unity when doing these cures.

Healing Energy

Natural beauty and healing energy are easy to add by bringing in fresh green plants (an odd number is good) or placing a colorful aquarium in the living room or family room.

✸ *Uplift the family by improving the general chi of family rooms.*

If your living room or den is a storage location for boxes or piles of undealt-with belongings, family chi can suffer. Old, heavy, and dark furniture can also add a heavy and depressing energy to your home. Removing these items helps uplift the energy and "makes room" energetically for the people again. See if you can replace what you remove with nothing or with something bright, fresh, and cheerful. When doing this, visualize that the old and hindering energy is leaving, and that new, fresh energy is invigorating your family.

✸ *Raise spirits by adjusting the "first thing seen" upon entering.*

An important factor for the overall Feng Shui of the household is the "first impression," or first thing you see when you enter the home. This principle applies to the main front door and to any side or garage door you enter often.

A positive image upon entering will bring peace and safety to the household. Plants, art, or objects of beauty are recommended. Visualize when you do this cure that the chi of everyone in the home is being stimulated and enhanced.

Method IV: Balance and Enhance Windows and Doors

✸ *Create harmony between parents and children with balanced window-to-door ratios.*

In Feng Shui lore, doors represent voices, particularly the voices of adults, while windows symbolize the voices of the children. If the voices of the children are ruling the house, compare the number of doors and windows you have. If windows outnumber doors by more than three to one, you've found a Feng Shui cause for the problem. The way to balance the condition of excess windows and create family peace is to hang a crystal ball or small brass bell in front of each window. This cure helps to "temper" the excessive chi of the windows. An alternate method is to hang a red silk tassel from each doorknob in the house to strengthen the chi of the doors, bringing their energy up to match that of the windows. Visualize family cooperation, harmonious communication, and peace reigning in the household.

⊕ *Eliminate discord and confusion by balancing misaligned doors.*

Another condition that generates disharmony and unbalanced chi occurs when two or more doors in a hallway are misaligned. A good cure for this problem is to hang a faceted crystal ball between the two doors. Be sure to hang your crystal from a red ribbon or cord that is cut to a multiple of 9" in length. Visualize that this cure creates harmony and cooperation for the occupants of the rooms and the family.

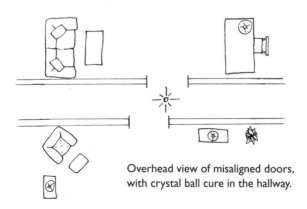

Overhead view of misaligned doors, with crystal ball cure in the hallway.

⊕ *Promote your family by harmonizing "clashing doors."*

Since doors represent voices, if a door in your home clashes with another door, arguments and family discord can result. Look for this condition in hallways where bedroom doors are located and in the Family and Children Guas. To harmonize the clashing doors, hang a red silk tassel from the doorknob of each door. Use this cure if your home feels as if it has "too many" doors. Visualize peace and cooperation in the family when you do this cure.

⊕ *Help voices speak by repairing doors.*

Occupants of households with Feng Shui door issues can experience emotional and physical speaking problems. To heal voices and enable them to speak the truth, fix all shortcomings of the doors in your house (see other door cures on pages 146–147). These cures are particularly vital for the Mouth of Chi (main front door) and master bedroom door, but are important for all the doors in the home. Your door cures will also enhance your personal energy and opportunities. As you perform these very important cures, visualize that you are now speaking the truth easily and with compassion.

⊕ *Empower children by fixing window problems.*

The same cures as given above apply to windows. Windows relate to the voices, self-expression, health, and well-being of children. Windows that are squeaky, stuck, painted closed, dirty, broken, hard to move, or have similar problems should be fixed as soon as possible for the welfare of your children and the overall chi condition of your home. As a part of this cure, visualize your children being free to grow and expand into their true natures.

8

Reputation and Fame

THESE CURES WILL HELP YOU enhance your reputation, your fame, how the community sees you, and your vision for your future. Reputation means what people are saying about you, and how many people are saying it. If actually becoming famous is important to you, the cures in this chapter will help that as well.

The part of your home's Ba-Gua that relates to both reputation and fame is called the Fame Gua. If you need to improve or increase the "word on the street" about yourself, this is the Gua to work in. Chi qualities to strive for in the Fame Gua include movement, openness, brightness, and upliftment.

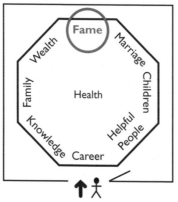

The Fame Gua

Method I: Brighten and Strengthen Your Fame Guas

The Fire element is associated with the Fame Gua, so bringing light, heat, or brightness into this Gua is a key method for increasing reputation chi in your environment.

⊛ *Brighten your reputation with a bright light.*

A bright light is a good symbol of fire energy, so adding a light to this part of the house will contribute brightness to your name. If you already have a light in this Gua, you can put in the brightest bulb possible or replace it with a stronger light. Using actual fire, such as with a fireplace or candle, is another good way to do this cure. As you do this cure, in your mind's eye see your reputation being spread brightly in the community.

⊛ *Create fame quickly with explosive power.*

Increasing your reputation and fame is the perfect excuse to pull out your handy string of symbolic Chinese firecrackers and hang them, using a red ribbon. These firecrackers can typically be found in Chinese gift stores or markets in metropolitan areas. (Symbolic firecrackers are not explosive or dangerous.) To fine-tune this cure, use nine (or a multiple of 9) firecrackers. When you hang your symbolic firecrackers, mentally see things "exploding in positive directions" for you.

⊛ *Boost your reputation with a mirror.*

Placing a large mirror in the Fame Gua is a good technique to draw more chi into the fame area of your life and magnify the energy already there. It is valuable when doing this cure to visualize the attraction and expansion of your reputation.

⊕ *Empower your reputation and fame with the color red.*

Red is the color of the Fame Gua, as well as the most renowned color used in Feng Shui. The presence of red in your Fame Gua will serve to strengthen your reputation. The color red can be added to the Fame Gua of your home, bedroom, office, or in all three locations. When performing this cure, visualize an expanding and powerful reputation.

⊕ *Add strength and righteousness to your fame with a flute.*

A bamboo flute will be your friend indeed for improving your reputation. The proper flute adds strength, uprightness, protection, and aus-piciousness: a great combination for enhancing your reputation. Be sure to use a flute that has its original bamboo segment ridges intact, not sanded off. If the flute is smooth, its power is diminished. (See page 72 for the type of flute to use and one way to hang it.)

Mentally visualize an increasingly positive reputation in your life.

⊕ *Generate reputation chi with powered items.*

Powered objects, such as appliances, can gen-erate positive reputation energy as well. You can put one in your Fame Gua, while visualizing that it is constantly generating a positive reputation for you. If you already have an appliance in your Fame Gua, make sure it is in good running con-dition and visualize it helping you create a pow-erful reputation.

⊕ *Get more people singing your praises with sound power.*

To increase your good reputation, a sound generator works well. Any sound-creating device can be used. Traditional options include the bell, wind chime, and gong, but modern variants work also, such as a tape player, stereo speaker, and telephone. Whichever option you choose, place it in the Fame Gua and visualize that the sound from this "generator" is going out constantly, reaching many people (both known and unknown), and creating a powerful reputation for you.

Method II: Stop Escaping Chi

⊕ *Stop escaping fame energy by "dispersing" the chi.*

A door or large window in the Fame Gua can allow fame, wealth, and health energy to leak out, especially if a path leads from the front door to the back door in a straight line. If your fame is lacking, this is an important point to check in your home. This "freeway of energy" situation can create "escaping chi," causing many negative life effects.

The preferred technique is to place a "dispersing cure" halfway between the front and back doors to disperse the energy coming in the front door into the rest of the home. This cure can be a hanging item, such as a wind chime, crystal ball, or mobile. If the space is large enough, a sitting cure, such as a plant, statue, table with flower arrangement, or other installation, can be used instead.

If the above option is not possible, a good substitute is to hang a chime or faceted crystal ball both just inside the front door and just inside the back door to hold the chi in the house and in your life.

Water Features in the Fame Gua

Since fire is the symbolic energy element for this part of your home, water, the element antagonistic to fire, can dampen your reputation if situated in this Gua. It is recommended to remove fountains, aquariums, and other water features you may have in this Gua. They can be replaced with one of the bright-energy cures found in this section.

For either cure, hang the item from a red ribbon that is a multiple of 9" long and mentally visualize the chi being spread throughout the house, feeding all areas of your life, especially those where you have a need.

Method III: Envision Your Future with a Treasure Map

⊕ *Reach your desired destination with a treasure map.*

Since the Fame Gua concerns your vision and projection of your future, it is beneficial to place a representation of your desired future in the Fame Gua of your home or bedroom. You can create this cure with a "treasure map": a collage made of photos, words, and other positive images of how you want your life to be.

Tapping into your right brain and creative awareness, a consciously created treasure map placed visibly in a Fame Gua is an excellent influence for your future. Written goals can also be placed prominently in this Gua. As often as possible, visualize this desired future occurring.

9

Helpful People and Friends

THESE CURES INVOLVE PEOPLE who are helpful to you, including friends, benefactors, and people who help you simply because they want to. They can increase the number of helpful people and friends you have. In this chapter, you will learn how to strengthen these important connections and make your network of friends stronger and wider.

Action, movement, and attraction are good energetic qualities to create in this Gua to draw more helpful people into your life.

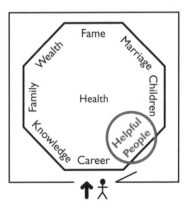

The Helpful People Gua

⊕ *Attract helpful people with a mirror.*

A strong mirror can be placed in the Helpful People Gua to pull in more people who are highly beneficial to your cause. For full effects with this cure, visualize helpers now being attracted to you from both expected and unexpected directions. (See mirror notes on page 50.)

⊕ *Generate more helpful people with a wind sock.*

A colorful wind sock or flag will add the energy of color and motion to this corner of your house and life. Hung outside, from a red cord or ribbon (cut to 9" or a multiple), this cure's color and motion generate active chi and helpful friends in your life. Visualize people being drawn to your cause in larger numbers.

⊕ *Activate your helpers by putting up their pictures.*

Another way to attain help in life is to place one or more photos of people who can assist you in the Helpful People Gua of your home or bedroom. Your picture can be greatly strengthened by attaching a 9" red ribbon (tied in a bow) on each picture. As you hang these pictures, visualize that they are coming to your aid now.

⊕ *Receive help by visualizing five helpers in your mind's eye.*

This cure is done purely on the mental level, yet is very effective if you practice it. To achieve a goal or receive help with a problem you face, see in your mind's eye the faces of five people who can assist you. See them helping you achieve your goals and needs. This cure will be strengthened if you perform it for nine consecutive days. It is further strengthened if you do it when going to bed, at the same time every night, for nine nights in a row.

⊕ *Gain more connections by adding moving water.*

According to the Five Element Theory, water in its moving state creates more connections with people. Therefore, a moving water cure is a good way to increase your network of friends and helpers. Put a fountain in the Helpful People Gua of your home, business, or office Ba-Gua. Occasionally placing a fresh green leaf in the water of the fountain can also assist your career. For greatest benefit, visualize that many people who want to assist you are flowing into your life.

⊕ *Increase help, luck, and protection with an aquarium.*

An aquarium is another excellent cure for your Helpful People Gua, assisting your luck, protecting you, and increasing the number of people who help you. The best number of fish is a multiple of 9. According to Professor Lin Yun, for more power, you can make each multiple of 9 contain eight red goldfish and one black goldfish. If a fish dies, it was protecting you from a negative event or attack. Replace any fish that die immediately to keep your aquarium at top effectiveness.

When you do this cure, see vividly in your mind receiving more help, having better luck, and being protected.

⊕ *Send out the word with the power of sound.*

The energizing power of sound can reach the people you need to contact. A wind chime in the Helpful People Gua of your bedroom, home, or office will send your message.

The best type of chime is metal, with a clear sound that you like. Hang your chime from a red ribbon cut to a multiple of 9" long. Your chime will be effective even if inside (not being blown by the wind). To actively boost this cure, you can ring it nine times on any day. Visualize the sound of the chime awakening many people who will come to your aid.

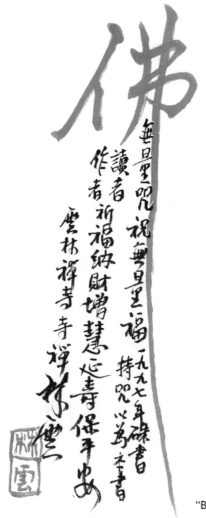

"Buddha"

10

Knowledge and Self-Improvement

THIS CHAPTER FOCUSES ON the inner areas of life: increasing your wisdom and intelligence and promoting your self-improvement and personal growth. These cures will build your "inner life": the world of study, reflection, and spiritual understanding. These values are cultivated by improving the Knowledge Guas, located in the front left area of your home, bedroom, and office.

Improving the chi of the Knowledge Gua and performing other knowledge and wisdom cures will help you:

- ▶ Increase your intelligence and intuition.
- ▶ Think more clearly with better decisions.
- ▶ Improve your self-esteem.
- ▶ Enjoy peace and tranquillity.

This is also a good Gua in which to do cures in order to increase your Feng Shui ability. All the cures in this chapter can enhance one or more of the qualities listed above. Your visualization, as always, will play a key role in strengthening the effectiveness of your cures.

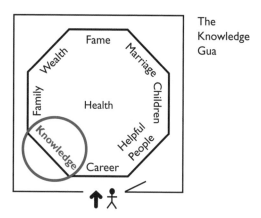

Method I: Brighten, Stimulate, and Awaken Knowledge Chi

⊕ *Brighten your mind with a light in the Knowledge Gua.*

The Knowledge Gua of the Ba-Gua is an especially good place for brightness cures. A bright light in the Knowledge Gua of your bedroom will have an enhancing effect on your intellect and awareness. As you perform this cure, visualize that bright, useful ideas are coming to you.

⊕ *Awaken more intellectual power by adding a wind chime.*

The awakening quality of sound can positively impact the mind in many ways. A wind chime or brass bell in your Knowledge Gua can act as an "alarm clock to the brain," waking up untapped mental potential. This cure can be placed in the Knowledge Gua of your home office or bedroom. When doing this cure, visualize your wisdom and mental energy awakening and growing.

◈ *Attract new sources of learning with a
   sizable mirror.*

If you want to attract new information on a
subject, a mirror will be your helper in the
Knowledge Gua. The power of the mirror combined with your intention will attract new knowledge and enhance existing knowledge. For this
cure, the bedroom is the most powerful location
to place your mirror, but the Knowledge Guas of
your house, study, living room, den, home
office, and work office are also good additional
locations. To maximize the power of this cure,
vividly see many new sources of learning
becoming available.

◈ *Grow new ideas and wisdom with a lively
   new plant.*

Plants are a strong source of new life and
healthy, vital chi. They are a great way of growing and strengthening the thoughts, concepts,
and answers you need.

A lush, green plant (newly purchased for this
cure) placed in the Knowledge Gua of your bedroom, home, or office will help you grow in
wisdom and understanding. Since blue is the Ba-
Gua color for knowledge, this cure will be
strengthened by using a plant that has blue
flowers. Make sure your plant stays healthy at
all times. Replace it quickly if it begins to wither.

You will empower this cure if you visualize
the plant's chi aiding your knowledge, with new
and effective ideas coming to you often.

◈ *Strengthen and protect your mind with
   bamboo flutes in your Knowledge Gua.*

Flutes are a powerful and highly recommended tool that can be used for cures in many
locations throughout your home. To strongly
enhance the knowledge sector of life, hang a

Calm a Chaotic Mind or Gently Stimulate Your Thinking

To stimulate your thoughts or to create greater calmness and peace of mind, several cures are available for the Knowledge Gua:

▸ Place a gently moving mobile in this location. Its circulating movements will activate new thoughts and concepts.

▸ Install a gentle fountain in the Knowledge Gua of your home or yard. The flow of the water symbolizes creative ability and new awareness.

▸ Put a clear pool of water in the knowledge corner of your yard. Still water represents the calm, mirrorlike nature of the mind.

For maximum benefits, clearly visualize your intended desire while performing the cure of your choice.

bamboo flute in the Knowledge Gua of your bedroom. (To ensure best results, see page 72.) Visualize that the flute is helping your mind be more strengthened and balanced.

⊕ *Activate your mind with moving objects.*

To "clear" cobwebs out of the gray matter, place a powered mobile object, such as a fan or kinetic (battery-powered) mobile or moving sculpture, in your Knowledge Gua. This cure can be done in the Knowledge Gua of your home, bedroom, office, or yard. Outdoor tools for this cure include brightly colored wind socks, pinwheels, and flags. Such cures combine the energies of color and movement to create a powerful stimulating effect.

Use positive visualization to stimulate the important inner elements of this cure.

Method II: Boost Personal Clarity with Crystals

⊕ *Enhance clarity of mind and decisions with a crystal.*

To enhance your mental clarity and expand your thoughts, an effective cure is to hang a faceted crystal ball in the Knowledge Gua of your home, office, or bedroom, or one in each place. For full effect, hang your crystal with a red ribbon, cut to a multiple of 9" in length.

As you put this crystal into place, visualize each facet of the crystal opening your mind to a new dimension of understanding and knowledge. See distracting, unuseful thoughts being swept away. Your mind is sharp and clear, helping you succeed in all parts of your life.

⊕ *Expand your knowledge with a crystal over your sitting position.*

To create overall benefit for your career, or to protect yourself from attack, hang a crystal ball (with a red ribbon, multiple of 9" long) over your head where you sit at your desk. This cure stimulates an expansion of knowledge and ideas, including clearer thinking, better decisions, and a brighter outlook on the future. As a part of this cure, visualize a newfound clarity of mind and that you are receiving the knowledge you need.

⊕ *Promote inner growth and peace with a crystal over your bed.*

A stronger variation of the above cures is to hang your crystal ball over the head of your bed. This cure will brighten your mind and help open more spiritual awareness. Other benefits of this cure include freedom from self-doubt, greater ease in getting to sleep, peaceful dreams, and a greater sense of calm and freedom. When you hang your crystal ball, visualize the benefits you desire occurring quickly and easily. Repeating your visualization before falling asleep each night will empower this cure even further.

Method III: Adjust Key Locations of Home and Office

In addition to doing cures in the Knowledge Guas of your home and bedroom, rooms associated with mental activity are important locations for making positive changes. Thinking patterns and mental habits improve automatically when rooms of the house and workplace associated with thought, reflection, and reading are adjusted with Feng Shui. These rooms include your desk, home and work offices, study, library, and living room.

✦ *Add positive chi by improving overall lighting in your knowledge rooms.*

Bright light adds positive chi, creating optimism and forward thinking. Dim lighting creates a somber, reflective, and possibly depressing mood. For a positive outlook on your future, windows and mirrors should be clean, clear, and unblocked by plants or other items. Visualize brighter thinking when you do this cure.

✦ *Increase mental energy with living plants.*

Living, growing energy feeds your mental energy and enhances the production of new thoughts. Use an odd number of fresh, new plants to enliven your knowledge and thinking powers. Visualize new, healthy thoughts growing in your life.

✤ *Clear your mind by reducing your furniture and household clutter.*

If there is not enough room to walk freely in your office or living room, chances are good that there are not many new and creative ideas springing forth from these locations. Too much furniture leads to too many books, papers, bills, and other unresolved piles of your life. The unfortunate truth is that most people have too much "stuff," the majority of which they don't truly use or need. A few creative types among us may thrive on a chaotic environment, but the rest of us are hampered when we're surrounded by tons of belongings. There's only one solution: Round 'em up and move 'em out! Visualize new freedom, openness, learning, and movement occurring in your life as you clear your space.

✤ *Reduce mental stress — organize or clear all unnecessary items.*

Not only is the amount of stuff you have important, but its state of organization is important as well. A desk and office in a perpetual state of chaos freezes precious brain circuits that must work overtime to handle the state of disorganization. The easiest, most powerful, and most important way to be more organized now is very simple: *Have less stuff.* It is virtually impossible to organize yourself if you have too many belongings.

It is helpful to realize that each unnecessary belonging holds part of your personal energy, both emotional and mental. Clearing out stuff you don't *truly* need returns that energy directly to you, increasing your vitality, freedom, creativity, and energy. A good rule of thumb is that if you haven't used something for six months, you probably never will. Recycle it ruthlessly and enjoy an easier and clearer life. As always, visualize clarity and increasing knowledge as you perform this cure. (See also "Cures for Clearing Clutter" on page 156.)

⊕ *Enhance family learning and study with visible books.*

A good cure to promote intelligence and increase everyone's desire to learn is to place books (neatly) so they can be seen immediately as you enter your front door. This first impression creates a reminder to learn and grow mentally. Visualize that this cure is helping you, and that knowledge and wisdom are growing.

Method IV: Use Knowledge Colors

⊕ *Empower your understanding with knowledge colors.*

Painting the living room a pleasant shade of blue or green can stimulate knowledge for everyone in the household. This cure also brings health, peace, and comfort to the house. In many homes, a white living room can be uncomfortably cool and a little sterile, not contributing to family unity and growth. Blue and green are also great colors for bedrooms; they add healing, peace, and new life, as well as stimulating intelligence and wisdom.

Visualize your desired results happening when you add these colors to your home.

11

Special Situations

THIS CHAPTER IS LOADED with many special cures you can use to adjust the chi of several important areas of your life:

- ▸ Improving luck and good fortune
- ▸ Travel
- ▸ Safety and protection
- ▸ Emotional strength and goal achievement
- ▸ Driving and your car
- ▸ Clearing clutter

Cures for Improving Luck and Good Fortune

⊕ *Increase your luck and protection with a Ba-Gua mirror.*

An excellent universal cure for good luck, great Feng Shui, and protection is to place a Ba-Gua mirror above your front door, on the outside of your house. A Ba-Gua mirror has a red and green octagonal frame decorated with the eight symbols of the *I Ching,* with a round mirror in the center. The Ba-Gua mirror represents balance in all areas of life, attracts auspicious circumstances, and protects the household against negative energy. When you hang this mirror, visualize the very best life has to offer coming your way this year!

A Ba-Gua mirror can be placed over the front door.

⊕ *Claim better luck and a better life by painting your door red.*

Having a bright red door can give your luck a needed boost, for red is the Feng Shui color with the greatest "auspiciousness" and "curing power." Since the front door represents the entire house, red at this key point bodes well for your fortunes, symbolizing an excellent future for the family. This cure is a good one to perform if you need a major life change, reversal of fortunes, or help from known and unknown sources. Be sure to visualize that the help you desire is coming your way and that you are being aided strongly by the power of the red color.

⊕ *Create smooth sailing when everything works smoothly.*

The working condition, status, and upkeep of all parts of your home are very important to pay attention to. Items that are broken, working poorly, or in a state of disrepair can bode ill for your luck and prosperity. Lack of maintenance creates subtle glitches that can pop up in unexpected and frustrating ways. Having broken belongings lying around, or stuffed out of sight in your basement or closet, symbolizes decaying energy — definitely not a desired state of affairs.

Feng Shui Cures and Broken Items

You can get a read on which part of your life is affected by a broken item in your house by checking the area of the Ba-Gua it resides in. Once you've fixed the broken item, you have just performed a cure for that life area! This cure is maximized if you visualize that you are achieving success in that area of your life.

Of particular energetic importance are any appliances, doorknobs, and other house features that seem to "resist" getting or staying fixed. The recommended path is to persevere until you have achieved victory. Your energy and your life are worth it, and you will most assuredly experience the benefits.

⊕ *Shift your energy by adjusting the color of your sheets.*

Your personal chi can be shifted in many ways by changing the color of the sheets on your bed. This simple cure is an excellent way to adjust your chi to help create your life goals.

Bedding Colors	Life Areas Cured
Pink	Relationships
Green	Healing, vitality, family, a new start
Yellow	Health
Purple	Wealth
Blue	Knowledge

Red is one of the strongest colors available for Feng Shui cures. Red sheets can be used as cures for healing, wealth, strength, and vitality. A key part of the bedsheet color–changing cure is to strongly and intently visualize your intended desire occurring when you put the new sheet color on your bed.

The Feng Shui Color Systems for Improving Luck and Having a Better Life

This all-purpose cure is designed to change your luck or give you needed help in any life area. Along with using individual Feng Shui color cures as covered in previous chapters, Professor Lin Yun teaches three additional methods for powerful use of color.

The Five Element Color System. This color system uses the colors that represent the Five Elements of Chinese energy theory (see page 88). The colors are black (water), green (wood), red (fire), yellow (earth), and white (metal).

The Six True Color System. The Six Color System uses white, red, yellow, green, blue, and black, which are called the Six True Colors in Tibetan Buddhism. When these six colors are used with a positive intention, they symbolize and project powerful healing and spiritual significance.

The Seven Rainbow Color System. The Seven Color System uses the seven colors of the rainbow: red, orange, yellow, green, blue, indigo, and violet. By using rainbow colors, you are covering the entire spectrum of visible light, thus symbolically "covering all bases" and asking for assistance from higher forces.

⊕ Using the Color Systems for Blessings and Benefits

You can place any of the color systems in any Gua in which you need to change or improve your luck. This cure method is quite versatile and works for virtually any life need. Since it creates balance using a variety of colors, it can be used for any reason and in any Gua in your home or office. The cure method is very simple: Choose the color system (Five, Six, or Seven

Color) that feels best for you. Place all the colors of your chosen color system in the Gua you wish to enhance. You can put one item containing all five, six, or seven colors in the Gua of need or place a separate item for each color in that area. If your color display is bright and eye-catching, it will be more effective than if it is small and hard to notice. Visualize blessings coming to you immediately and continuously. See the colors you have chosen making your desires come to pass quickly and easily.

You can apply this cure in multiple ways throughout the house; each time you install your colors, be sure to see in your mind your luck improving and positive events coming your way.

⊛ *Create good luck by wearing the Five, Six, or Seven Colors for special help.*

With a little ingenuity, the above cure can also be applied to the clothing colors you wear. If you need special assistance from "higher sources" on a particular day, increase your likelihood of receiving it by wearing all the colors from one of the three color systems. You can use a separate clothing item for each color (not all colors need be visible) or you may wear one article of clothing (shirt, blouse, for example) that has all the colors in it. Best results come when you match the colors exactly to the systems given above.

These color schemes may or may not fit into your fashion regimen, but can prove very effective in changing your luck and fortunes. Be sure to visualize your desired goals occurring as you wear the colors you have chosen.

Cures for Travel

⊕ *Retain your energy by choosing your hotel room carefully.*

When traveling, your chi can be weakened by long hours on the road or in the air. Your need for balance and rest increases at these times. One of the chief cures to use on the road is to choose carefully the hotel room you stay in.

Many hotels and motels have varying floor plans for their rooms. Some people have found that they look at several rooms in a hotel before finding the most suitable one. If you are sensitive to noise, seek a room away from traffic, elevators, and vending machines.

⊕ *Have a good stay — choose a room with the bed in a Commanding Position.*

For the most powerful and protected feeling, it is best if the bed is farthest from the door and you can easily see the room door when lying on the bed. If you are in a suite, make sure the bedroom door is visible from the bed. Also desirable is to ensure that the door path doesn't run directly across the bed. (See several Commanding Position guidelines for optimum bed placement on page 64.) This cure is maximized if you visualize your trip being auspicious and fortunate.

⊕ *Feel safe by making a hidden door visible.*

Many hotel rooms are designed so that you cannot see the door while lying in bed. If this is the case, you are in a weaker energy position. This position creates subtle or overt feelings of unease and lack of safety. This situation can sometimes be solved. For example, a mirror can be positioned on the floor, a table, or a chair at an angle that allows you to see the door from the bed. For best results when performing this cure, visualize enhanced safety and control over your circumstances while traveling.

⊕ *Enhance wealth with a mirror in the wealth corner.*

Wealth can be empowered by putting the mirror in the wealth corner of the room, an especially good cure if it coincides with the above cure. Visualize increased wealth as you reposition the mirror.

⊕ *Travel safely by bringing your crystal ball.*

Carry a faceted crystal ball with some red ribbon and thumbtacks. The crystal ball can be installed over your head in the sleeping position (from the wall is usually easiest). The crystal will have the effect of balancing the chi over your head, creating peace, balance, and smooth thinking. This is an all-purpose travel cure. When using it, visualize any goals you wish — clarity, good rest, safety, auspicious travel, and/or wealth.

⊕ *Increase safety and alertness with a brass bell.*

Another good carry-along cure is a brass bell. A bell can be hung from the room's doorknob as an added safety cure or hung in front of a corner that is aimed at the bed. When you place your bell, visualize increased safety and balance.

⊕ *Zap EMFs before they zap you.*

Electrical appliances can zap the body's energy fields. Be sure to move electric alarm clocks, radios, and other appliances at least 24 to 36" away from your sleeping position. Another option is to use the wake-up call or a battery-operated alarm clock so you can unplug all electrical appliances at night. The television is an especially insidious radiator of electrical fields. You will more rested when it is unplugged from both the electrical and cable outlets. Visualize enhanced health when doing this cure.

⊕ *Retain personal chi by closing drains.*

Close the bathroom door and all sink and tub drains in your hotel room. As you seal the drains, visualize that your personal chi is retained. (See page 83 for more drain-sealing cures.)

Cures for Safety and Protection

⊕ *Strengthen psychic boundaries and self-protection with mirrors.*

Mirrors are a strong helper for keeping yourself protected from the unwanted thoughts, feelings, and projections of others. This cure is good for threats on a physical, psychic, or spiritual level. One application is for neighbors who harbor ill will. *Note:* Use this cure only with compassion and for self-protection, never to "direct" energy toward another person.

A mirror can be placed on the outside or inside of the house on the wall nearest the trouble zone, with the reflective side of the mirror toward the negative energy source. Another way to do this cure is to place your protection mirror anywhere in the Gua most associated with the troubled area of your life. Octagonal mirrors are especially powerful for this type of cure. When you do this cure, be sure to visualize that a clear and powerful boundary has been set, and that you are safe and protected.

✦ *Add protection and a royal touch with Fu Dogs.*

If you feel the need for protection, another cure is to place a pair of Fu Dogs or Lions outside the front door of your house. These creatures are the Chinese lions or lion-dog beasts seen sitting outside of Chinese restaurants and shops. Their regal bearing and ferocious nature symbolically frighten any negative energies or individuals headed toward you. One should be placed on each side of the Mouth of Chi, or main entrance.

Larger and better-quality lions are stronger. Sources for Fu Dogs or Lions include landscaping stores, lawn or garden ornament outlets, and Feng Shui mail-order catalogs.

When you install your guardians, they will be the most helpful if you visualize that they are protecting you and guarding the property.

✦ *Add protection with firecrackers near your front door.*

An excellent cure to add protecting energy to your home and life is to hang a bundle of Chinese artificial firecrackers near the front door. Your firecrackers can be just outside the front door. (If you live near a Chinatown, you can get symbolic firecrackers at many shops there. These firecrackers will not actually explode.) Visualize the symbolic "explosive" power of this cure warding off negative spirits, people, and events.

Cure for Emotional Strength and Goal Achievement

✷ *Claim personal power by enhancing the center.*

The center of the home or bedroom is a key location to adjust in order to enhance your inner personal strength, including emotional strength. This is also a good location for cures that improve self-esteem and self-worth. A wind chime or a faceted crystal ball can be hung with a red ribbon (cut to 9" or a multiple of 9) in the center of your home or bedroom. When you do this cure, visualize your inner core being strengthened and your emotions being balanced.

Cures for Driving and for Your Car

✷ *Create safety and ease of driving with a crystal ball.*

You can enhance your car's energy and your driving comfort by hanging a faceted crystal ball from the rearview mirror. Use a red ribbon with your crystal for greater effectiveness. See your life and your car being protected and blessed whenever you are behind the wheel.

✷ *Bless your car with a red string on the steering wheel.*

A simple method Professor Lin Yun teaches for help behind the wheel is to tie a 9" length of red ribbon onto your steering wheel. When you place this cure, visualize that you are always headed in auspicious directions while driving and in your life.

⊕ *Simplify your life with a car that is clean and working properly.*

Your car's working condition and appearance can be either a positive, contributing factor or a detracting, debilitating influence on your personal chi. If your personal chi needs a boost, take a good look at your vehicle. If it needs to be cleaned or fixed, your chi will be positively affected by doing so. When this cure is performed, visualize a smooth flow of energy and success in your life.

Cures for Clearing Clutter

If you have a specific pile or stack of clutter that doesn't seem ever to get dealt with, Feng Shui has some helpful tips. The following cures are for spaces that get cluttered with changing items and for specific piles of the same stuff that stay put and resist getting cleared.

⊕ *Cure the clutter with a roving wind chime.*

A wind chime is a helpful friend in time of need for your clutter woes. Hang a nice-sounding metal wind chime with a red ribbon over the pile of greatest distress. Visualize that the sound from the chime creates a positive whirlwind blowing through your clutter and cleaning it up for good. You may be surprised to see that later in the day or the next day you have newfound energy to go after this pile once and for all.

After this location is clear, the wind chime can be moved on to the next pile that needs attention; repeat the cure as above. Keep your eye on the first location: If it starts to fill up again, you may need to keep a permanent chime in that location.

⊕ *Start the change with just one piece to cure the clutter.*

This cure is good for a cluttered space that is quite daunting even to begin clearing. The technique is very simple: Just dispose of a single item from the pile, no matter how big or small your pile is. Each time you pass this clutter, see if you can clear one additional item. Reinforce each action with visualization. The key to the effectiveness of this cure (like all the cures in this book) is in the visualization. See in your mind's eye that the energy of the space in need has now completely changed, with pieces starting to move on their own to their appropriate file, box, or trash can.

⊕ *Handle clutter for good by putting it on wheels.*

Sometimes the clutter won't move simply because it's been in the same place for too long and has grown roots. This cure is for the stuff you really don't want to deal with, now or later. First, use both of the above cures on the clutter. If you need more horsepower, put the pile of clutter on a cart or dolly and move it to another part of the house. Move the cart to a new place each day for nine consecutive days, each time visualizing that it is getting easier and easier to take care of.

By the end of the ninth day, either it will be quite easy to handle or you could be willing to chuck the whole mess — wondering why you didn't do so a long time ago!

12

Enhancing Your Cures

IN THIS CHAPTER YOU WILL LEARN principles and techniques that will strengthen your Feng Shui cures and life changes.

A special technique Professor Lin Yun teaches to enhance your cures is the "Three Secrets Reinforcement." The Three Secrets is an integral part of each cure and is essential for creative and successful cures.

In this book, strong emphasis has been put on using visualization within each cure to create your desired results. However, visualization is just one of the Three Secrets. Using all three together yields a much greater effect. The Three Secrets are: *Body Secret* (sacred hand position), *Speech Secret* (prayer or mantra), and *Mind Secret* (visualization). (*Note:* In this context, "secret" means "powerful inner method.")

The Three Secrets Explained

⊕ *The Body Secret*

The Body Secret uses a sacred hand gesture to align your body's energy. The hand gesture recommended is the Expelling Gesture, performed by flicking the middle and ring fingers out from the palm.

The Body Secret: beginning and completion.

The flicking motion is done nine times in a row, with the left hand by men and the right hand by women. (Nine symbolizes completion and achievement.) This motion expels blocks and hindrances from your life and welcomes the positive benefits you want. Using another sacred hand gesture is fine, such as the prayer position (hands together) or any other meditative hand position you prefer.

⊕ The Speech Secret

The Speech Secret empowers your cures with sacred speech, such as prayer or mantra. The Speech Secret uses the powerful energy of your voice to strengthen the cure. The recommended sacred speech to use is the "Six True Syllables": **Om Ma Ni Pad Me Hum** (pronounced ohm-maa-nee-pahd-mee-hum). This ancient prayer creates balance, harmony and compassion. You can also use another word or prayer such as Om, Amen, the Lord's Prayer, *peace,* or *love.* The effect your sacred speech has on you is more important than the exact words. To perform the Speech Secret, repeat your sacred speech aloud or to yourself nine times.

⊕ *The Mind Secret*

The Mind Secret is visualizing, a powerful and effective method of creating life change. In this step, you realistically visualize the events, conditions, and scenes you desire in your life. You can use the visualizations suggested for the cures in this book, or use your own. The clearer your mental pictures are, the better. See what you want so realistically that it feels like it's happening right now.

Keys to Effective Visualizations

Professor Lin Yun teaches two important visualization tips:

Visualize in detail. See your desire occurring in as much detail as possible.

Visualize in three stages of development: (a) See the beginning: the start of what you want. (b) See the middle: the continuation and improvement of your desire. (c) See the culmination: the positive achievement of your desire.

Performing Cures with the Reinforcement

Now here's how to put your whole cure package together:

1. Make the physical change in your space: Hang the mirror, place the fountain, etc.
2. Perform the Three Secrets Reinforcement in these three simple steps:

REINFORCEMENT	ACTION
Body Secret	Perform flicking motion 9 times
Speech Secret	Repeat sacred speech 9 times
Mind Secret	Visualize your desired results happening

Five Important Principles for Your Feng Shui Success

Here are five important principles you can use to make your Feng Shui cures and life changes more tangible and immediate:

1. **Urgency.** Do your cures as soon as possible once you recognize the need for them. It is recommended that you perform your cures within three days of recognizing the need for them, if possible.
2. **Involvement.** Do each cure completely. Put forth your best effort and intentions. Throw your whole self into it and you'll be sure to get the best from your cure.
3. **Sincerity and Expectation.** Do all your cures with a sincere attitude for best results. Believing that your cures are working helps change the chi of your life.
4. **Higher Guidance.** If you feel stuck or unclear about something in your Feng Shui, ask for Divine guidance from the Source you feel most connected to: God, Jesus, Buddha, Allah.
5. **Perseverance.** Continue doing cures! Feng Shui is an ongoing process, not a one-time experience. The more cures you do, the more your home will support your desires. As you continue making changes, you may notice new areas of your home that need attention "popping up." Go after them with gusto!

Index

Note: Page numbers in italic indicate illustrations.

About the Author and His Teacher

Professor Thomas Lin Yun, Ph.D. (left) is the leader of contemporary Black Sect Tantric Buddhism, an author, a lecturer, an artist, and a distinguished philosopher. A world authority on Feng Shui and Chinese culture, Professor Lin lectures extensively at the invitation of leading universities and religious organizations worldwide. To receive a schedule of Professor Lin Yun's activities, please contact:

Yun Lin Temple
2959 Russell Street
Berkeley, CA 94705
510-841-2347

David Daniel Kennedy (right) is an ongoing student of Professor Lin Yun. He teaches Feng Shui classes internationally and designs custom training programs for Feng Shui practitioners. He is a columnist for *Natural Health* magazine and *Feng Shui Journal,* and is a featured speaker at Feng Shui conferences worldwide. He is available for residential and commercial Feng Shui consultations.

To learn more about Feng Shui and items for your cures, or to arrange a Feng Shui consultation or receive the author's schedule, please contact:

Int'l Institute for Grandmaster Lin Yun Studies
PMB 127
1563 Solano Avenue
Berkeley, CA 94707
Toll-Free: 1-888-470-2727
Fax: 510-237-7374
Web site: http://www.fengshuiweb.com
E-mail: dkennedy@earthlink.net

Other Storey Titles You Will Enjoy

The Feng Shui Garden, by Gill Hale. Teaches how to create balanced outdoor spaces that positively influence health, relationships, and happiness. 128 pages. Paperback. ISBN 1-58017-022-6.

Keeping Life Simple, by Karen Levine. Offers hundreds of pertinent ideas about how to create a lifestyle that is more rewarding and less complicated. 160 pages. Paperback. ISBN 0-88266-943-5.

Keeping Work Simple, by Don Aslett and Carol Cartaino. Provides practical tips for simplifying any work environment to achieve maximum performance. 160 pages. Paperback. ISBN 0-88266-996-6.

Tips for Your Home Office, by Meredith Gould. Includes advice for creating the most comfortable, professional, and productive home office environment. 160 pages. Paperback. ISBN 1-58017-003-X.

Be Your Own Home Renovation Contractor, by Carl Heldmann. Explains finding and appraising a restorable structure, obtaining financing, and hiring subcontractors. 176 pages. Paperback. ISBN 1-58017-024-2.

Be Your Own Home Decorator, by Pauline B. Guntlow. Provides step-by-step instructions for redecorating any area of your home regardless of budget or experience. 144 pages. Paperback. ISBN 0-88266-945-1.

These and other Storey books are available at your bookstore, farm store, garden center, or directly from Storey Books, 210 MASS MoCA Way, North Adams, MA 01247, or by calling 800-441-5700. www.storey.com.